CLICKING WITH GOD

Jon Riley

Copyright © 2012 by Jon Riley

Clicking with God
by Jon Riley

Printed in the United States of America

ISBN 9781625091987

All rights reserved solely by the author. The author guarantees all contents are original and do not infringe upon the legal rights of any other person or work. No part of this book may be reproduced in any form without the permission of the author. The views expressed in this book are not necessarily those of the publisher.

Unless otherwise indicated, Bible quotations are taken from The Holy Bible: New International Version. Copyright © 1996 by Zondervan.

www.xulonpress.com

I wish to dedicate this book in memory of my spiritual mentor and dear friend Daniel D. Wilkinson, Ph.D. I was adrift on the stormy seas of college life, and you instilled a Christ-like calm for which I will be forever grateful. While you were taken from this life far too soon you remain my model of what it means to click with God. See you in Heaven!

> Therefore, since we are surrounded by such a great cloud of witnesses, let us throw off everything that hinders and the sin that so easily entangles, and let us run with perseverance the race marked out for us. (Heb. 12:1)

TABLE OF CONTENTS

INTRODUCTION xi

PROLOGUE xvii

Part I: Problems, Pitfalls and Predicaments! 23

Chapter 1 25
The Problem of Authenticity

Chapter 2 35
A Problem of Perception

Chapter 3 47
The Problem of Perfection

Chapter 4 57
The Problem of Self

Chapter 5 69
The Problem of Sin

Part II: The Path of Promise 85

Chapter 6 87
Putting First Things First

Chapter 7 95
Choices, Choices, Choices

Chapter 8 105
From In Adam to In Christ

Chapter 9 117
Walking with Christ

Chapter 10 127
Dancing with God

Chapter 11 135
Running the Race with the Holy Spirit

PART III: PRACTICING HIS PRESENCE 147

Chapter 12 149
Living in the Third Dimension

Chapter 13 161
Living Dangerously

Chapter 14 173
Living in His Fields

EPILOGUE: IT'S OUR TURN NOW 183

INDEX 191

Acknowledgments

I wish to thank the following people who provided love, encouragement, patience and insight to make this book a reality.

. . .you, the reader, may the words of this book guide you to the one Word which matters – His!

. . .Dave Tubbs. Your enthusiasm, candid feedback and input have all been an inspiration to me. For the past 20 plus years you have been more than a friend; you are a mentor and a Christ-like example.

. . .Pastor Troy Ogle. More than anyone you took the time to listen and give me scriptures to explore. Your insights were fundamental in helping me see the direction God desired me to take in writing this book.

. . .my eight year old son Patrick, without whose loving attention this book would have been finished in half the time.

. . .my wife Alice, without whose loving attention and support this book never would have been finished.

. . .Him! May I always be in His fields working in rhythm with my Creator!

Introduction

Habituation. There is a word you don't hear every day. Have you ever searched the house for your glasses, only to discover you were wearing them? Have you ever looked for your set of keys, only to realize they were in your hand? These are examples of things we become so comfortable with that we forget they are even there! Habituation is an extremely simple form of learning in which we, after a period of exposure to a stimulus, stop responding. It is analogous to wearing glasses... or a retainer. Now, there is an unpleasant memory. When I first got my retainer, I would constantly fidget with it. Initially it was uncomfortable; it didn't *feel* right. I would continually adjust, readjust, pop it in and pop it out, which inevitably led to breaking it – much to my parents' chagrin. However, over time, my body adjusted to the point where wearing my retainer felt normal. In fact, I would forget it was even there.

Habituation: the first five letters are h-a-b-i-t. Good habits are often hard to start and bad ones are almost always hard to break. If these habits are sinful, not only are they hard to break, they are lethal. I am not a pastor. I am not a degreed theologian. I am the guy you sit next to at church. I am a Christian who has strived to listen to God and follow his path for most of my life. For the past 20 years I have served in various positions: from boards to teaching Sunday school classes, to leading the teen group and various other roles of servitude at the four churches I have been lucky to call home. However, Satan is not easily defeated. He continually probes and pokes looking for our areas of weakness – our Achilles heels. He found mine. If he hasn't already, he will find yours.

This book is not about going into the gory details (or not so gory, depending on your opinion about those things) of my sin. People are funny when talking about sin. Their sins are never as "bad" as the other guys' sins. What some consider a "major" sin, you diminish as an error in judgment. Well, the fact is I've sinned and I still sin. It's not like I woke up one morning and decided that I was going to sin. It was more subtle than that. I didn't so much fall, rather I slowly slid into a pit I didn't even realize I was in until it was too late. I had become comfortable with my sin. I was able to continue to go to church, teach and serve on the board. My sin became a habituation.

As you read this book, you will come across many of the lines I have used in my teaching over the last 20 years. Phrases like "earn the right", the "twelve inch journey" and "clicking with God". How ironic that my sin was eroding the very Christian life that I held so dear. I had become comfortable with a sickness in my life. It was a disease that was growing and continuing to manifest itself in more and more destructive behaviors. It had become a corrupting force, subtly wreaking havoc in my spiritual life. How did this happen? What could I do to right my course? Did I even want to? Let me take you back to my turning point.

It was the fall of 2005. I had an appointment the next morning with my Pastor to discuss my desire to go into ministry. Can you believe it? I was thinking about being a Pastor while hiding a devastating secret. God intervened. That night God revealed the totality of my sin and its impacts to those I loved most. What a horrible and yet wonderful experience. The overwhelming realization of my sin was like a tsunami. The first three verses of Psalm 77 completely capture my despair that night.

Introduction

I cried out to God for help; I cried out to God to hear me. When I was in distress, I sought the Lord; at night I stretched out untiring hands and my soul refused to be comforted. I remembered you, O God, and I groaned; I mused, and my spirit grew faint.
Psalm 77:1-3

It was not an enjoyable evening, yet it was the beginning of true repentance, grace, forgiveness and healing. The next morning I did go to meet my Pastor . . . to confess . . . and to agree that whatever I believed my call may be regarding being a pastor my first call was to be obedient to God. He was speaking, and I needed to listen, repent and respond to His call to follow Him.

As I struggled to fully grasp the road ahead of me I slowly came to the realization of another, deeper, underlying issue I had been unknowingly struggling with for years. It was not a "sin", but rather a misunderstanding of what it really means to be a Christian. Later in the book I will talk about speaking at a youth retreat where God began to reveal this misunderstanding to me. I was trying to reconcile calling myself a Christian while struggling with sin. Shouldn't mature Christians get to the point where they no longer sin? Some of you, I am sure, do not struggle with this "theology", but I did. Somewhere in my Christian journey, my desire to become a more mature and "sanctified" Christian had become equated with "sinlessness". This belief was not holding up to personal experiences, so I had three choices: live with the guilt of sin I could not conquer on my own, become comfortable with it to the point where I no longer acknowledged its impacts on my life and those around me, or walk with my Savior and begin to understand the depth of His grace and my need to respond in obedience to Him daily.

Changing bad habits is hard. So is conquering the effects of sin. Thank God (literally) that He does all the heavy lifting. Actually He does all the lifting. Unfortunately Satan did not simply give up and go home that night in 2005. He is still the prowling lion (1 Peter 5:8). He is the great deceiver. He still tempts and lures. However, my journey with God that began that night has revealed to me the extent of His grace and that Christ's power of forgiveness and strength to walk with Him is exceedingly greater. For the next few years I began again to walk with God. Some days we could run and some actually felt like we were dancing. But on others I continued to trip and fall. However, Christ has been by my side, walking with me. Sometimes with an outstretched hand to lift me up and forgive me, while all the time making sure I am fully aware of my weakness and His strength.

Just over a year ago I was sitting at my kitchen table. It was very early. I was doing my devotions and trying to decide what exactly God had next for me. Should I start a new adult fellowship class at church? Should I write original material for a Wednesday night bible study? How about starting a small group in my home? It was during this time of reflection that I felt a gentle nudge to write a book. I have never written a book. While I had been encouraged by several people over the years to write a book I was not sure. Was this something God wanted me to do or something I desired? I reached out to several very dear Christian friends to pray with me about the project. More than a few have been instrumental in the final product you now have in your hand.

My next question was what to write about. Several ideas came to mind. Making a long story short none of them ended up being completely on target. It was not until I began actually writing that God led me on a spiritual journey that has ended with a story about my experience that wonderful and horrible night six years ago. I have always believed in relational evangelism and discipleship. It was key relationships with strong Christians that laid the foundation for my faith in Christ. However, I had fallen away from what I had always coined the "Twelve Inch Journey" where we apply what we "know" to how we live. It is when Christians are truly able to take this short journey from their head to their heart that they

Introduction

experience God in a way where we "click", but I am getting ahead of myself.

As I was writing it became clear that I was exploring the edges of those "beliefs" I had about Christianity that had created an area of confusion, of misunderstanding, where Satan began subtly attacking. I needed to peel back the layers of what exactly I believed and determine if it was actually Biblical. I needed to fully grasp the truth of what God desired of me and truly begin clicking with God. This book attempts to capture this journey in a way that I hope will be applicable to your life.

This book is about clicking with God. It is based on what I have learned during my struggles with faith – and ultimately, my understanding of God's call on our lives. It is about discovering that God is not necessarily calling us to some sinless life of perfection, but rather to a life of obedience . . . one choice at a time. It is about a loving God who is more gracious than we are flawed. God desires to walk with us. He desires for us to click with Him. He is calling us to responsibly accept His free gift of grace and become transformed. Only then will we discover the beauty and utter fulfillment of clicking with our Heavenly Father.

If you are a Christian this book is for you. So many of us are "good" people – attending church, maybe even brought up in the church, but we have settled for "Sunday Christianity". God is calling His Church to be more than a Sunday morning ritual. We are called to a life that clicks with God. If you believe you have reached a point where you are beyond God's grace - this book is for you. If you are a Christian who thinks you are beyond sin this book is also for you – maybe mostly for you – because you are standing where I once stood.

Pride, self-confidence and an "I can do it myself" attitude comes before the fall – I know.

In His Fields,

Prologue

Meet The Weavers

Has your family ever been mistaken for the Cleavers? You remember, June and Ward? *Leave It To Beaver*? It is hard to claim to be American and not have seen at least one rerun of this classic sitcom which aired in the late 50s and early 60s. Six full seasons of Theodore "Beaver", his older brother Wally and their parents have made them the idealized suburban family. I bet they never had a Sunday morning like most of us experience almost weekly.

Does this sound familiar? Let me introduce you to the Weavers. Sunday morning; 8 AM, somewhere in America. Bob Weaver is dressed in his standard Sunday garb - dark slacks, crisp white shirt and tie. He is positioned on his traditional perch – the black leather recliner in the den. With one hand he finishes off his second cup of coffee while the other effortlessly manipulates his smart phone. As he puts down the coffee cup he reclines on his throne and begins monitoring the sounds of his family getting ready for church. His serene weekend morning is about to take a dramatic (and typical) plunge into chaos.

Leslie Weaver is in the kitchen, still in her robe, getting a casserole ready for today's potluck. Oh, and she is maintaining the silent treatment with Bob that she initiated the evening before when he had failed to address the still leaking faucet in the master bath. By the accusations and commotion audible from upstairs you will recognize that two kids are awake, but more interested in their share of the mirror than actually brushing their teeth.

Now, the words fashionably late are not in Bob's vocabulary, and he has no intention of being late for church on this, or any other, Sunday morning. "You kids have exactly five minutes to be downstairs and dressed for church!" Bob sternly calls out in the direction of the staircase.

"I don't know what to wear Daddy," his 7-year old daughter responds.

"Ask you mother," he shouts back making sure Leslie can hear his impatience.

Several moments of silence follow until, with a clang of pans in the kitchen, Leslie whisks by without even a glance and storms up the stairs. What is heard next is a volley of commands and complaints as she tells her daughter that she *will* be wearing the pretty new dress, and then pleads with her 10-year old son to put down the video game, brush his teeth and to put on something presentable.

"You now have four minutes. Don't make me come up there," Bob threatens.

Several minutes later the daughter, in her dress, comes moping down the stairs clearly unhappy with the situation, followed by her brother wearing jeans, a tee-shirt covered with battling aliens, and still playing his video game.

"Put that away before I throw it away! And you are *not* wearing those clothes to church young man," the father bellows. "Get back upstairs this instant and put on something appropriate. Your mother will help you."

The boy slowly turns around, defiantly drops his game on the couch and stomps up the stairs making sure every step is as loud as his mismatched socked feet can make.

"Your nice tan pants are hanging in your closet! You can get them yourself. I am curling my hair," Leslie calls out to her son, her voice echoing through the house.

"Daddy, I am hungry," states Bob's daughter.

"You are a big girl now. Get some cereal from the cabinet and milk from the refrigerator," he states without even glancing up from his smart phone which he continues to feverishly attack now with both thumbs.

The next few minutes proceed in relative silence. Bob gives the Sunday paper a quick look, glances at his watch and stands up to get a final cup of coffee. "It is now 8:30 and we need to leave in 15 minutes!" he exclaims.

Ten minutes later the son comes back downstairs and plops at the kitchen table noticing that his sister is using his bowl for breakfast. "That is my bowl," he exclaims and begins to reach to reclaim his property.

The sister shrieks in objection and quickly pulls the bowl back towards herself and in the process empties the entire contents down the front of her dress. The next several moments are a blur of crying, yelling and finger pointing. Bob, waving his finger in the air, yells out that he has finally reached the limits of his patience, while his son cowers at the kitchen table and his daughter runs to Mom.

"What happened?" Bob can hear Leslie say to their daughter. "That is going to have to be dry cleaned! Take it off, we will find something else for you to wear."

"We need to be leaving right now!" Bob pronounces to no one in particular as he heads out the door to the garage.

Ten minutes later Leslie and her still sniffling daughter come back downstairs. Bob is sitting in the car in the driveway getting angrier by the minute while his ignored son has resumed playing his video game. Leslie grabs the casserole and a couple of granola bars to eat in the car, calls to her son to put down the game, and takes her daughter's hand as they move towards the car.

As everyone climbs into the running car Bob doesn't even attempt to hide his frustration as he drums his fingers on the steering wheel as everyone gets seat belted. "We needed to be at church five minutes ago," he announces as he abruptly puts the car in reverse.

The children sit momentarily silent in the back seat while Leslie sits down in front with the casserole on her lap. As Bob begins to back the car out of the driveway she remembers she forgot her Bible. "You did that on purpose," Bob says under his breath as Leslie hops out to run back into the house.

After she returns with both her Bible and the kids offerings, Bob backs out onto the street while Leslie opens up a granola bar for her breakfast.

"I am hungry," the daughter says.

"Me too," adds her brother.

Leslie closes her eyes, clenches her jaw, takes one bite out of the granola bar and then hands the rest of it to her daughter and the other to her son while mumbling, "I hope they have bagels at church."

For the next fifteen minutes the family drives in silence while the kids eat and the parents stew. As they round the final corner to church Leslie quips, "The bathroom faucet is still leaking."

Bob clenches his teeth but does not respond. His sharp turn into the church parking lot says it all. "I knew it," Bob says. "Just great. We are late *and* our parking spot has been taken. Just great!"

Bob finds another spot a good twenty feet further from the side entrance, pulls in, abruptly stops, opens his door and gets out without another word. The children hop out and the son bolts for the door where his best friend is waiting. Leslie, casserole in one hand and Bible in another, walks alongside her skipping daughter - both trailing Dad by a good 10 feet as he briskly approaches the entrance.

As they approach, the doors are opened by a well-dressed greeter who offers a warm smile and a handshake. "Well, if it isn't the Weaver's. How are you doing Bob?" the greeter asks.

"Couldn't be better," he lies as he firmly shakes the greeter's hand. "It is a great day to be in the Lord's House."

As they walk down the crowded hallway Leslie shifts into church mode and lovingly announces so others can hear, "Honey, I am going to drop off Suzy at Sunday School and this casserole in the kitchen. I will meet you in class downstairs."

Without stopping Bob responds, "Thanks dear," and he makes his way to their Sunday School class on the lower level. He enters to find a handful of young married couples already congregating around the coffee and donuts someone thankfully brought. Mr. Weaver, all smiles and handshakes, walks to the front of the class he and his wife facilitate and quickly scribbles some Bible references on the whiteboard which outline today's discussions about love – *loving God and loving others.*

"Now where is my Bible," he wonders.

PART I

PROBLEMS, PITFALLS AND PREDICAMENTS!

OUR BARRIERS TO CLICKING

Chapter 1

The Problem Of Authenticity: Dangerous Masquerades

"Illusion is needed to disguise the emptiness within."
Arthur Erickson

Can anyone hide in secret places so that I cannot see him?" declares the Lord. "Do not I fill heaven and earth?" declares the Lord.
Jeremiah 23:24

Jesus answered, ". . .Everyone on the side of truth listens to me." "What is truth?" Pilate asked
John 18:37-38

*I*f you have children and attend church I would assume that you have experienced some form or fashion of the Weaver's story from the Prologue, Meet the Weavers. As a friend of mine is prone to say, "Sometimes we almost lose our religion just trying to get to church." Now, I will be the first to admit that my home is not immune to this problem. However, instead of going into graphic, self-incriminating detail allow me to share a "safer" illustration.

Make believe is one of the all-time favorite past times for children worldwide. My son is no different. Many of his games of make believe often end with the exclamation, "Tricked you!" It is the exception that a day goes by without our son attempting to make a piece of silverware magically "disappear" into his hand (we pretend we don't hear it hit the floor), telling a vivid story of his mysteriously new found super powers or an animated display of the just discovered ability to use "the Force." He is quite theatrical, but always looking for awestruck incredulousness in the faces of his audience. Once achieved he stops, points a victorious finger at us and says those two magic words - "Tricked You!"

How often are we dissatisfied with our lives? And how is this even possible? We are the wealthiest, most pampered humans that have ever lived in all of recorded history. I'm going to go out on a limb here and postulate that we are dissatisfied because we are striving for the world's values. We want acceptance, or wealth, or power, or friends, or fame, or any other square peg for the round hold of discontentment.

The Weavers want to keep up with the Cleavers. We seemingly always yearn for "something more" and fail to actually believe Jesus when he tells us that our highest value is to obediently act on our opportunities to love God as well as the guy (or gal) next to us. Because, let's face it, we are swamped with those opportunities daily.

Just this morning my son said he dreamed he could fly. Not with a jet pack but just like Superman. How cool would that be? We often do not like feeling limited, constrained and trapped. So we choose to put on masks of superiority, infallibility, and far too often self-righteousness. We strive to imitate those we view to be perfect. Far too often they are those "photoshopped" megastars gracing the television screen, magazine covers and billboard. Unfortunately they also include those apparent "Super Sunday Christians" intermingled with the "normal" flock of our Church communities. Talk about masquerades! These pretentious facades are but the hopeless imitation of a false center. Yet Paul is very concise in his letter to the church at Ephesus that there is only one true center, he states:

> Be imitators of God, therefore, as dearly loved children and live a life of love, just as Christ loved us and gave himself up for us as a fragrant offering and sacrifice to God. (Eph. 5:1-2)

Why do we struggle to consistently imitate God? Why do we so often masquerade at church? Why do we fail to live out our Christianity at home, school or work? Do we really think we can "trick" God? As I revealed in the Forward, these are questions I have struggled with in my own life for years. The greatest challenge facing the effectiveness of Christ's Church is our inability to live out our faith in our homes, in our neighborhoods, in our schools and in the workplace. The old adage that "seeing is believing" is unfortunately almost never true. Authenticity comes with the baggage of over exposure. If

The Problem Of Authenticity: Dangerous Masquerades

anything, the norm is to be non-authentic. We see it in politics, Hollywood, advertising, and our churches.

Advances in computer rendering and image enhancing tools such as Photoshop make it possible for anyone with a computer to manipulate video and images. The advertising world has been doing this for years— sacrificing integrity to sell you a story and reap the monetary rewards. You can be pretty much assured that every image you see in a magazine or lofted up on a billboard has been <u>significantly</u> altered and enhanced to appeal to the most people. Photographs, once lauded for authentic snapshots of a moment in time, rarely represent reality anymore.

As Christians, what is the "picture" we attempt to portray to the outside world? How would we like people to see us? Is it love? Or is it someone striving for acceptance, wealth, power, friends or fame? What I find disturbing is how I fail to effectively and consistently portray my Christian faith during the week. Too often I struggle at the grocery store with the slow checkout lines or at work with the guy in the next cube who is clearly not carrying his weight. I struggle driving when that loving soul in front of me didn't hit the gas so we could both make the light. I struggle at home to consistently love my family when crises hit - especially on Sunday mornings! Let me tell you something - people are watching the "picture" you are painting every day, every moment. When we struggle to consistently and effectively live out our faith people see it. They hear it. They remember it.

Now I am not about to start talking about living "perfect" lives. We will cover that trap in another chapter as we continue to peel back the layers of the very real problem facing all of us who call ourselves Christians. If we claim to be Christians, if we want those around us to associate Christianity with how we live, we must be willing to authentically display Christ at work in us. That may mean that we temper our responses with an attitude of Christ. It may mean that we need to seek forgiveness when we have not. If those around us see nothing different in our lives they will see no relevance in Christianity, or worse they will secretly call us out as another example of the biggest problem with Christianity – hypocrisy. When people claim to be Christians but clearly don't act Christ-like, when we preach one thing but live something entirely different, we fall into the trap of hypocrisy. It is the greatest tool Satan uses to undermine the Church.

The term hypocrisy is primarily limited in the Bible to the New Testament. In the original Greek the word denotes a masked actor. They were pretending to be something that they were not. If you want to see just how big an issue this is to Christ's Church simply Google "Christian Hypocrisy" and you get nearly 6 million results. During one search the first result was an article titled "Christians are hypocrites". A quick peak at the article yielded the following quote, "The problem with their approach lies not only in an oft-noted failure to practice what they preach, but an equally pronounced tendency to ignore what the Bible itself, preaches."[1] *Bing* the same two words and you get another 5 million results! Almost in response to the above quote Bing's first result is an article discussing hypocrisy in the church. A quote by Ravi Zacharias quickly grabbed my eye when he states, "The Bible's condemnation of hypocrites is clear. The Bible also clearly pledges that God will judge hypocrites" (Matthew 24:51). God is more angered by hypocrisy than we can ever be."[2] It is a popular phrase to say the least. It is a devastating phrase that is crippling the Good News.

Our ability to live a life of Christian love is strengthened when we learn to authentically lean on and support other believers within The Body – the very definition of the Church. However, Christians are experts at pretending everything is OK. I have often wondered if it isn't some kind of spiritual "gift". Often times I wish I was able to do this better. It is apparently a communication skill that I am only beginning to fully master. My tendencies to wear my emotions on my sleeve severely hinder my abilities to effectively hide much of

---

[1] http://www.evilbible.com/christians_are_hypocrites.htm

[2] http://www.christiananswers.net/q-aiia/hypocrisy.html

The Problem Of Authenticity: Dangerous Masquerades

anything I am feeling. Most people who know me, and in fact most who do not, would say it is very obvious if I "feel" OK or not. So, in an attempt to improve my abilities of self-deception and non-authentic self-portrayal I considered auditing an online course titled "An Introduction to Self-Delusion" (yes, I am making this part up!).

The course is critical for those of us who find ourselves all too often in situations where everything is spiraling out of control, but we don't want the outside world to know the true anxiety, hopelessness or guilt that we feel. The course is set up to give us the tools to protect ourselves and project to the outside world the image of a carefree happy person. These methods take time to learn, but once mastered you may not even know for yourself how you truly feel. The four tools of self-delusion are quite simple.

The first is to always smile. Keep it in place at all times. Give others the impression that you really are happy. Be overly happy, almost to the point that you are manic. Annoy people with the fact that you never seem stressed or sad. The second tool is to have an escape plan. It is critical for the successful self-delusionary individual to find a place to go where you don't have to deal with reality. This place doesn't have to be an actual location. It can be in someone's arms, into a book, or even into another state of mind. Third, lie. Lie to everyone, especially to yourself. This is very difficult at first. But eventually, with enough practice, you will be able to have no idea exactly how unhappy you truly are. Finally, don't think. Until you master the art of lying to yourself, just don't think about anything. Don't think about the topics that will bring you down, and don't think about anything else either since your thoughts may wander down paths to the topics that are depressing. So, to be safe, just don't think. Now, as with any powerful set of tools a warning is in order. If done for too long, one may lose the ability to feel real happiness.

Until we deal with the tendency towards non-authenticity we will continue to go to church and hide our struggles by flipping the "happy switch". We will continue to go to church and "smile" making sure everyone believes everything is OK. I don't presume to think this will be anything but difficult and challenging for all of us to change, we are after all human. Deepening the challenge is that most of us have, unfortunately, become experts in the art of self-delusion. We put on our happy face, lie to ourselves that everything is OK and hope that the other smiling Christians – many of whom are also masquerading – don't notice the hurt, pain, guilt, confusion and other personal struggles lurking behind the façade. The goal is not to go through the motions, survive another Sunday and escape back to our homes, jobs, or wherever else we don't need to keep up the act. We continue to masquerade at church and struggle in life.

I will be the first to admit that we have, unfortunately, very good reasons to not transparently reveal our weaknesses in church. Like any large gathering of people, "The Mob" can be brutal. Judgment is rife in our churches and retribution could be devastating. If I show my dark side in a place where God is "supposed" to help you eliminate the darker aspects of our human nature, I'm liable to be exiled. While we come to church seeking authentic faith, hope and love (1 Cor. 13) we too often perceive an almost unaccepting spiritual elitism. Note that I said perceive, the vast majority of Christians do not intend to be perceived this way, yet we often are. Too many Christians believe that if we don't put on the mask on Sundays, someone will judge us for not seeming "Christian enough".

There is an inherent sense of fear of non-acceptance, fear of condemnation, a feeling of guilt that inhibits our ability to be a part of the fellowship of the Body of Christ. There remains a lurking belief that we must be "perfect". After all, didn't Jesus say, "Be ye holy; for I am holy?" (1Peter 1:16) The damage this expectation of perfection creates can be tremendous. In our churches the fellowship that God intends for the Body of Christ is not being fully realized because we are not authentic – we pretend that we have arrived at perfection instead of agreeing together that we are all on the journey toward perfection – and that none of us has arrived. Even the most "veteran" Christians fall prey to this trap.

We feel the subtle pressure to conform to some unspoken level of "acceptable normalcy" at church, and this normalcy has very little room for those brave Christians who actually reveal their anxieties, struggles and weakness. We gladly sing the old hymn "Just as I Am" knowing God offers His grace to all of us just as we are, but when we walk out of the sanctuary we revert to hiding who we actually are, from our fellow Christians. If we cannot be authentic at church how can we ever be the hands and feet of Christ living authentic lives that call us to love our neighbor as ourselves? Authenticity is difficult. It is frightening. It is far easier to point the finger at others, criticizing their failings. We ridicule others to feel better about our own areas of weakness. Max Lucado wrote, "A church will never die from the immorality in Hollywood or the corruption in Washington. But it will die from corrosion within — from those who bear the name of Jesus but have ever met him, and from those who have religion, but no relationship."[3]

So, what about your life? Your actions? Your walk? Stop settling for the masquerade. Begin to experience the authentically joyful life as you click with God. We are called to be the light and the salt of the world. We are called to be the hands and feet of Christ. We are called to be the Church, Christ's Church! We must strive to consistently and authentically reflect the One we claim to follow. Let's choose to break this cycle and move forward along a trajectory of grace and victorious living that God calls us to journey. Let's recognize and accept His solutions for our struggles, and obey His call. Our best opportunity to reenergize our faith and improve our saltiness is through true fellowship with fellow believers where we authentically share our walk – both our struggles and our praises. If there are places where you are challenged or feel guilt, find that trusted fellow believer and be true. Account-

---

[3] Lucado, Max: *Life Lessons from the Inspired Word of God: Book of Romans.* Dallas, Tex. : Word Pub., 1996 (Inspirational Bible Study Series), S. 22

able authenticity will help you mature into the Christian God has called you to be.

With that said I will be the first to admit that practicing this is anything but trivial. First, the larger the group the more unlikely authenticity and accountability become – Christians and non-Christians alike. The reason this is so difficult is that people are more interested in justice than grace. We need love not a lecture. Authenticity is nurtured as we foster accountability with those core few (or one) Christians. If we fear rejection or judgment we will temper our level of honesty. Secondly, authenticity does not happen overnight, even with our closest friends. I will talk later in the book about "earning the right", but for now remember that accountable authenticity requires a marathoner's approach. This is not a sprint. You must be in it for the long haul. And please remember that true accountability focuses as much on what we should be doing as on managing the sin. Finally, as Christians we must put off self and put on Christ. The secret to living an authentic life is not striving to live a "perfect" life, but by living Paul's "life of love". This is what I call "clicking" with God. So, how do we click with God? How do we get in step with God? Well, first we need to live authentically, but it is more than that. We also need to recognize that how we perceive our faith, understand biblical perfection, view our self and acknowledge our sin are four other problems that become snares and pitfalls keeping us from clicking with God.

Chapter 2

A Problem Of Perception: What Does Christianity Look Like?

"All our knowledge is the offspring of our perceptions."
Leonardo Da Vinci

"Christianity has not been tried and found wanting; it has been found difficult and not tried."
Gilbert K. Chesterton

"Then Barnabas went to Tarsus to look for Saul, and when he found him, he brought him to Antioch. So for a whole year Barnabas and Saul met with the church and taught great numbers of people. The disciples were called Christians first at Antioch."
Acts 11:25-26

I once read the phrase *truth is universal, but perception of truth is not*. Perception, what I perceive to be true, can be referred to as a notion, a thought, an impression or an image. So what is my perception of Christianity? When I say I am a Christian what am I really saying? How do I know I've correctly understood, with my little, human, gray matter brain, the ineffable, infinite, timeless God of the Universe? The debate defining Christianity is as old as the religion itself. What do we believe? The fancy word for this study is theology. You can't have Christianity without Christ, yet Christ has been the center of controversy since He walked the shores of Galilee. So who is Jesus? Human, deity or both? What is his relationship with God? How does your perception of truth impact your responses? What difference does it make for your life?

300 years after Christ's life, the turmoil surrounding these very questions came to a head. Some denied Jesus' humanity while others denied His deity. A third group "reduced" His deity, while a fourth "reduced" His humanity. Other groups formed even more ideas, more perceptions. To address this threat to the Church (and to attempt to give his rather fractured empire a common religion) Emperor Constantine convened the Council of Nicea in 325 A.D. The most significant result of this meeting was the first uniform Christian doctrine, called the Creed of Nicea which would later (381 A.D.) become adopted at the Council of Constantinople as the Nicene Creed. This statement of core Christian beliefs was intended to establish orthodoxy (right beliefs) and bring unity to the Church.

As I read the Nicene Creed or the similar Apostle's Creed, I find myself immediately in agreement. I suppose this is not surprising, since I was raised in a Christian environment, built on these core values. However, a radical commitment to live a life that pleases God requires me to ask myself: Does my mental assent to these doctrines equate to Paul's "life of love" discussed in the last chapter? Does my head knowledge translate into heart action? How do I perceive myself when I say I am a Christian?

In his classic book, *The Cost of Discipleship*, Dietrich Bonhoeffer coined the phrase *cheap grace*. He writes "cheap grace is the preaching of forgiveness without requiring repentance, baptism without church discipline, Communion without confession. Cheap grace is grace without discipleship, grace without the cross, grace without Jesus Christ."[4] In a very similar fashion, Christianity has become cheapened. In the United States we look for "blue light special" Christianity. We want a drive through church, we want to take away as little as possible so we can exit through the Ten Items or Less express checkout. We want to be able to walk away feeling better about ourselves without any hint of accountability. For many that is what is meant when they say they are a Christian.

According to a 2008 Gallup poll[5] 93% of Americans celebrate Christmas and nearly 80% call themselves Christians. While these numbers support the notion that America is still a Christian nation, if we look a little deeper what we find is cause for concern. Of those Americans who call themselves Christian only 6 out of 10 "regularly" attend church. Less than half view their faith as important in their daily lives or believe Christianity can answer today's problems. Gallup has been collecting this same type of data for over 60 years. These most recent results represent a new all-time low with this troubling downward trend expected to continue. One question this poll does not address is what does one mean when they say

---

[4] Bonhoeffer, Dietrich. *The Cost of Discipleship*. New York: Macmillan, 1966.

[5] http://www.gallup.com/poll/124793/this-christmas-78-americans-identify-christian.aspx

A Problem Of Perception: What Does Christianity Look Like?

I am a Christian? The problem begins with the fact that today the word Christian has become nearly emptied of its true meaning – to be an obedient follower of Christ. Too often the term Christian is generically applied to any American who is not Jewish, Muslim or atheist. We must first be reminded that its original meaning is a noble one, one of which any follower of Christ can rightly be proud.

The word Christian appears a mere three times in the New Testament (Acts 11:26; 26:28; 1 Peter 4:16). In each instance, the word Christian assumes that the person called by the name was a follower of Christ. Christians were loyal to Christ, just as the Herodians were loyal to Herod[6] (Matthew 22:16; Mark 3:6; 12:13). The name Christian most likely originated with either the Greeks or Romans as a means to identify the followers of Christ in Antioch. While it was probably an early form of derision and a label which could earn you a death sentence, Christ's followers turned the tables and used it themselves as a name of honor, not shame. To be a Christian requires a level of identification with Jesus. It is more than just intellectual acceptance of facts or simply agreeing that Jesus existed. It is more than just going to church or living a *good* life. Christians are to die to the old way of thinking, but then become alive to a new way of living. Followers of Christ are not just people who abstain from sin, but are people who enter into God's service and manifest His Kingdom here on earth! Defined simply, but accurately, a Christian is someone who has decided to entrust his or her life as a follower of Jesus Christ and to live out their life as Jesus would have lived it. A Christian trusts Christ for forgiveness of sin, a right standing before God, and guidance in life. You can't take "Christ" out of Christian.

With that said what does being a Christian look like? If you were to draw a picture of your relationship with God what would it look like? What is your perception of your

---

[6] Youngblood, Ronald F.; Bruce, F. F.; Harrison, R. K.; Thomas Nelson Publishers: *Nelson's New Illustrated Bible Dictionary*. Nashville : T. Nelson, 1995

faith? Several years ago I was speaking at a youth retreat outside Kansas City. During our first evening together the youth pastor asked each of his teens and leaders to draw a picture depicting how they viewed their relationship with God. I will admit that I thought this was a bit corny, a picture of my relationship with God? Kind of abstract don't you think? Part of my skepticism was founded in my complete lack of artistic ability. How do you illustrate a relationship? For some it may be a picture of them kneeling at the foot of the cross. For others it may be the image of them walking with Jesus down a tree lined path. While for others it may not be something so pleasant. It was kind of a tough assignment to start a retreat off with, but better them than me. If nothing else it gave me a few extra minutes to review my thoughts and key points for that evening's opening discussion.

For the retreat I developed a series of discussions that centered on something I call "The 12 Inch Journey". The 12 inch distance is a crude measure of the distance between your head and heart. The discussions are meant to form the steps in a journey moving teens from just knowing about God (head knowledge) to living for God (heart living), from simply going to church to being the Church, from a life without God to a true relationship with Christ. In a word to be a Christian! It then struck me that, perhaps, this abstract exercise to illustrate your relationship with God was the best first step to begin the journey. It wasn't long before I would learn the depth and insight of the exercise. The youth pastor distributed paper and pencils to the group, and I sat back and waited while they worked on their "assignment". It was not long before one of the teens approached me and asked if I was going to draw my picture. To be honest I was a bit perturbed. After all, I was the speaker. And as I mentioned earlier, I don't fancy myself an artist. However, in that moment I recognized that these teens did not know me at all. I was a total stranger asked by their youth pastor to come and speak at their retreat. If I was going to ask them to listen to me and engage in the journey I first needed to earn their trust. So I reluctantly agreed to take a swing at illustrating my relationship with God.

As I grabbed a clean sheet of paper and a pencil I realized that I had no idea where to begin. "What does my relationship with God look like?" As I pondered the question a memory from college quickly surfaced. While at the University of Illinois I had been exposed to Campus Crusade for Christ. They have a simple, wonderful series of images outlining three types of people: Self-centered, Self-directed or God-directed. For each of these there is a very simple image:

THE SELF-CENTERED LIFE
The self-centered life is a person who has not received Christ. This person is not a Christian. Self is in charge with Christ completely on the outside of his or her life. The various interests of this person, represented by the various sized circles are totally self-directed.

THE SELF-DIRECTED LIFE
The self-directed life looks similar. The person has accepted Christ into their life and they are a new Christian. Self is still on the throne and Christ is not yet allowed to direct his or her life. In their own power the new Christian attempts to do the right things, failing to lean on the power of Christ.

THE GOD-DIRECTED LIFE
The final type is the God-directed life. This is the life completely directed by Christ. Christ is now on the throne and we completely and consistently yield to His Lordship.

What are your initial thoughts when you look at these images? If we are honest with ourselves we can all relate with the first image. All of us, at one time or another – maybe still today – remember our lives before Christ. Many of us may see ourselves as self-directed Christians – babes in Christ. However, very few of us, if we are honest, readily see our lives as completely and consistently God-directed. The majority of Christians would say they continually vacillate between God-directed and Self-directed.

Do any concerns arise when you look at these images? When I have asked this question to Christians the primary response has been their perception of the near impossibility of completely and consistently living out a God-directed life. These three distinct images seemingly convey distinct and somewhat instantaneous changes of state, but are they correct? While many of us agree that when we accept Christ, we are changed from self-centered unbelievers to Christians. Most, if not all struggle with the instantaneous change from being self-directed to totally God-directed. Can this actually happen in a moment? Is it even possible? The challenge arises in our perception that this final image conveys a kind of Christian "perfection". Hold that thought because we will get to that "problem" in the next chapter. I will admit that this same perception has proven to be a real problem for me, a stumbling block. While my relationship with God had definitely matured beyond the Self-Directed Life, I had a very difficult time viewing my relationship as completely and consistently God-Directed.

Something was missing in these images. Something was not quite right. I am at a youth retreat, getting ready to speak to a roomful of teenagers and youth leaders, and I begin to sense God speaking. He was gently uncovering a very real problem in both how I viewed and how I lived out my relationship with Him. This was more than a year before my turning point encounter in 2005 that I talk about in the Forward. God was working in my life, attempting to reveal Himself to me. So there I was, about to lead a weekend retreat

A Problem Of Perception: What Does Christianity Look Like?

discussing the "12 Inch Journey" and it became very clear that my journey needed to be reenergized, renewed. To be honest my initial reaction then was to minimize the moment. Yes God was speaking, but it was more about what I was going to say than how God wanted me to live in relationship with Him. After all, I attended church every Sunday morning and every Sunday night, even every Wednesday night. I was a teacher, youth worker and served on the church board. Isn't that what it means to be a Christian? While in my head I knew that Christianity was much more, I had become satisfied with a shadow of the true relationship God desires.

Becoming a Christian involves the spiritual, physical and mental turning from self to God. This is the very essence of repentance. By faith we believe that Christ comes into our lives, forgives our sins and begins to transform us into what He created us to be. There is a very key word in the last sentence that is the essence of my problem – *begins*. Looking back at the images depicting the self-directed life and Christ-directed life I don't see the process of *becoming* Christ-directed, I see only an event. According to these images one moment I am self-directed, the next I am God-directed. I recognized, for the first time, that my journey, my walk with God is in this in between. With that I drew this image to describe how I viewed my relationship with God. I believe that Christ is on the throne of my heart. He has access to every room of my life. As he uncovers those messy nooks and crannies, collecting  all of my day to day junk and those hidden corners of disobedience and sin, Christ begins the process of calling me to obedience. In many of those areas I readily trust and obey. However, there are still places where I attempt to hang on to my own self-directedness. While God may be on the throne in most areas of my life, there still are times where I clutch the throne, struggling to obediently let go.

Now, do I really want to share this revelation with a bunch of teens whom I've just met? What will they think? Will I lose credibility? What will others at the church think or the people that invited me? Should I simply act as if I am fully Christ-directed? Herein lies the deeper problem and a big reason many Christians, including myself, prefer to masquerade at church. I will tell you that I shared the image. I will also tell you that this image became an acceptable image of my relationship with God. Not acceptable in the fact that it was acceptable to God, but that I became comfortable with that depth of relationship. I accepted the fact that this was "as good as it gets." What is also interesting is that the temptation to hide behind a mask of "perfection" was totally unnecessary. My fears that I would somehow lose credibility with the teens, youth leaders or pastor were baseless. If anything, being honest about my relationship with God, with my struggle to let go, laid the foundation for a very effective weekend with all of them.

Looking back over the past several years I will also tell you that I have had those gentle nudges, "feelings" that there was something more to my faith, more to this life that I was failing to experience. I felt that God was calling me to take the next step with Him. He was calling me to something higher. He was calling me to let go. Off and on I would sense these callings, struggle to understand what they meant, become frustrated that nothing was happening and eventually lapse back into complacency. It was not until God revealed the depth of my problem that wonderful horrible night in 2005 that I began to realize that my inability to deepen my relationship with God was completely tied to the problem in my illustration. How can Christ be on the throne when I continued to cling to it? The words "No Lord" cannot go together. Clinging to the throne represents disobedience – sinfulness. I needed to take a good hard look at my relationship with God and with His help deal with the underlying problems.

A Problem Of Perception: What Does Christianity Look Like?

What I have discovered is that there were problems understanding and accepting my true relationship with God. My authenticity, my perceptions of perfection, self and sin were keeping me from continuing to be transformed. It is in fact these barriers that God had been revealing to me that were keeping me from taking that next step to a deeper relationship with Him. Before we move on to tackling these problems I want to challenge you to take a moment and reflect on your relationship with God. What does it look like? How would you illustrate it? Spend some time reflecting on how God wants to deepen His relationship with you. Where is God calling you out of your comfort zone? Where is God calling you to a deeper obedience, to a stronger love? If you will honor God with your time I am confident that God will reveal how He wants to move in a relationship with you.

Chapter 3

The Problem Of Perfection: It Is All Greek To Me

"What is perfected hereafter, must be begun here."
Benjamin Whichcote

"They say that nobody is perfect. Then they tell you practice makes perfect. I wish they'd make up their minds."
Winston Churchill

"Be perfect, therefore, as your heavenly Father is perfect."

Matthew 5:48

*F*aultless? Fat Chance. Flawless? Forget it. Impeccable? Impossible. Perfect? Please! Yet isn't that exactly what Jesus is saying during his Sermon on the Mount when he says, "Be perfect" (Matthew 5:48)? As one of my mentors is prone to say, "Either it is true or false." When someone intimates that they are in some way perfect we would say that they are arrogant, self-deceived and proud. I have no problem with Jesus being perfect, but me? I was raised in a tradition that uses phrases like "Christian Perfection" and "Entire Sanctification". They are freely sprinkled into sermons and Sunday School lessons, but I never completely understood their Scriptural foundation. I found in my Christian walk that *perfection* was a very dangerous word — a stumbling block that I misunderstood when I left it devoid of its Biblical context. It became a real problem. However, when I consider my true situation, this call of Jesus became an announcement of God's gracious plan for my life – for all of our lives.

Let's review our situation. We are all faced with the universal problem of self-centered lives, sin. It is sinful man who has fallen and is separated from God (Romans 3:23; 6:23). However, as Christians we know that Jesus is God's provision, His only provision, for this problem of sin. Through Jesus we can know and experience the love of God (Romans 5:8; John 3:16). However, it is not enough just to know this truth, even Satan knows this (James 2:19). We must accept this free gift of grace from God. This is the point where Christ enters our life and we move from self-centered to self-directed, the second image in the previous chapter. But we must also accept Jesus Christ as our Lord and Savior. It is only then that we can know and experience God's love and plan for our lives (Eph. 2:8-9; John 1:12). This is the truth captured in the image of the God-directed life.

Becoming a Christian involves the spiritual, physical and mental turning from self to God. This is the very essence of repentance. By faith we believe that Christ comes into our lives, forgives our sins and desires to transform us into what He created us to be. This transformation is a process. Academically I can agree with this fact. However, looking back do I really believe this truth? It is wonderful head knowledge that I can communicate during a lesson, but has it fully taken root in my heart? Deep down I have struggled to accept anything more than an event. And in doing so I am prone to fall into the trap, the lie of absolutism, perfectionism. When we fall into this trap we see the God-directed life as static, a status beyond which no further development, no further transformation is required. We see it as a "perfect", sinless relationship. It is something out of reach, not meant for this side of Heaven. Now I have heard many learned Christians, whom I respect, endlessly debate this notion of perfection and it seemingly always spirals into a debate about what is sin. Much of this debate hinges on whatever definition the debater deems accurate. We will cover the problem of misunderstanding sin in Chapter 5.

However, in avoiding this trap of perfectionism or absolutism I don't want to stray too far and stumble into a pit of ambiguity. Those mired in ambiguity stop striving for a life that is God-directed. Today, too many Christians live by the slogan "Nobody's perfect." We not only accept imperfections, we settle for "good enough." Both of these responses fall far short of a life that is clicking with God. So, what did Jesus mean when he said, "Be perfect?" Every now and then a good word study is necessary, and, since I just said that, you might guess that I think this is one of those instances. What did Jesus really say? What did he mean? What was the context of this statement? And how is this word used in the rest of the Bible? The answers may surprise you.

In her Biblical survey of "perfection"[7] Mildred Bangs Winkoop thoroughly details the attributes of the English word "perfect" and the difficulties they bring to this discussion. She correctly states that in English "perfection" is associated with flawlessness, impeccability and faultlessness. Applying these associations to the Biblical text tends to obscure the specific meanings and their nuances in the original Greek. In all there are five Greek words that can be found to be translated "perfect" in the New Testament. Four of these words do not refer directly to redemptive truths. They respectively mean *fitted or qualified, diligent or accurate, made full, and fitted together or properly adjusted*. However, when the New Testament writers speak about the redemptive concept of perfection they use the word family - *teleios* which is derived from *telos,* typically translated *maturity or completion*. It is always in reference to that which has reached a completion consistent with an intended end. It is this word that Jesus uses in Matthew 5:48, and one of the few places where it is translated "perfect", at least in the NIV. To summarize, there are two distinct yet coupled "perfection" messages in the New Testament. The first relates to the perfection of the Cross as completely fulfilling the new covenant. The second refers to the process of maturation to which Christ calls all Christians.

Let's look at these one at a time and then study two distinct examples where Christ discusses these truths. The first concept of an achieved perfection is dramatically communicated by the author of Hebrews.

> Because by one sacrifice he has made perfect forever those who are being made holy. (Heb. 10:14)

Christ offered one sacrifice, Himself. His job was complete! It is finished! It is for all time! It is perfect! It is by this perfect

---

[7] Wynkoop, Mildred Bangs; Beacon Hill Press: *A Theology of Love.* Kansas City: 1972, pp283-286.

(*complete, finished*) offering at the Cross, that Christ creates the bridge to relationship with God. Christ says this himself when He calls out from the cross, "It is finished!" (John 19:30). In the original Greek the words used both in John for "finished" and in Hebrews 10:14 for "perfect are from the Greek word *telos*. In both cases Scripture is saying that everything that had to be done has been completed so that we, through Christ (Eph. 2:8), can be made righteous (Rom. 5:19)! Finally, it is important to note that it is not the offering that perfects, but rather it is Christ Himself. It is Christ who has made us *complete, finished*. Everything that needed to be done for us to be in a right relationship (righteous) with God has been completed. There is nothing that is still required to have that relationship except to receive the free gift of what Christ has already provided. At that moment we are restored to a right (righteous) relationship with God. Our standing before God has been restored to the relationship God originally created us to enjoy. But this is not the end of the story, but rather only the beginning.

Paul and the author of Hebrews use variations of *telos* on several occasions to illustrate the second "perfection" message when they contrast maturity (*perfection*) with immaturity or even childishness. In his first letter to the church at Corinth (1 Cor. 2:6; 3:1; 14:20), Paul admonishes the presumptuous, immature Christians. While they thought they were spiritually mature Paul had to remind them of their vanity. While they should have matured (become perfect) they remained morally deficient (childish). Notice the difference in tone between Paul's contrasts in his letter to the church at Ephesus (Eph. 4:13-14) (positive encouragement) versus Corinth (like scolding a child). In each case Paul is contrasting perfection (maturity) with childishness. Finally, the author of Hebrews uses the word in a fashion identical to Paul's. (5:13-14). In all these occasions maturity (perfection) is equated with moral character and spiritual responsibility. On the other hand, the child is someone refusing to grow up, pathetic spiritual irresponsibility. I have a eight year old son. I expect him to act eight years old. I don't expect him to act eighteen, nor do I allow him to behave like a three year old. The same is true in our spiritual lives. God does not accept anything less for us spiritually.

So, we can see two sides to the perfection coin: Legal & Spiritual and Absolute & Relative. Legally and absolutely when we accept the gift of grace we enter into a relationship with God which is perfect (*complete*). Spiritually we are perfect as we mature in our walk with Him. This perfection is the pursuit, the journey toward Christian maturity. So the two sided coin says, "You are a Christian, now be one!" Paul gives us a wonderful personal example in his letter to the church at Philippi. As a bit of background, this church was heavily influenced by Greek philosophy. Many young believers were assuming once saved they would live happily ever after. This led a false sense of security, a type of perfectionism where they saw no need for either spiritual development or some cases spiritual behavior. Paul refuted this with vigor.

> Not that I have already obtained all this, or have already been made <u>perfect</u>, but I press on to take hold of that for which Christ Jesus took hold of me. Brothers, I do not consider myself yet to have taken hold of it. But one thing I do: Forgetting what is behind and straining toward what is ahead, I press on toward the goal to win the prize for which God has called me heavenward in Christ Jesus. All of us who are <u>mature</u> should take such a view of things. And if on some point you think differently, that too God will make clear to you. (Phil. 3:12-16)

In verse 12 Paul clearly writes that he has NOT "already been made perfect" but instead states his desire to "press on to take hold of that which Christ Jesus took hold of me." The perfection he desires is Christ's-likeness. This is not a goal we will ever *flawlessly* (perfectly in the English sense) achieve this side of heaven. It is a goal that is always just out of reach. Nevertheless, it is this goal, this ideal that God calls us towards. The perfection Paul is pursuing with all his might is translated as "maturity" above which is demonstrated by the pursuit of the perfection he denies to have already attained. Listen very carefully. Perfection is NOT an achievement but rather the pursuit of maturity. It is not static but dynamic. In the Bible perfection is a relational term. It does not necessarily mean mistake free or flawless. Instead it is about surrender and obedience. It is not about a finalized condition but a life lived out each moment to the level of Christ-like maturity that grace has granted.

So with all of this as background let's revisit what Christ says about perfection. In Matthew we find a young man asking Jesus the way to eternal life. Jesus answered, "If you want to be perfect, go, sell your possessions and give to the poor, and you will have treasure in heaven. Then come, follow me" (19:21 NIV). Here Jesus uses for perfect *telos* the same Greek word used by Paul and the author of Hebrews. Using what we just learned, Jesus is saying, "If you want to be spiritually mature. . ." But there is more here than meets the eye. Jesus is the master teacher. He is pulling this young man out of his comfort zone. He is calling him to grow. Let's go back and look at the previous portion of the discussion. Christ's first response to the question (v. 17) is to simply keep the commandments. By this Christ is referencing the Ten Commandments. This is not about simple law-keeping but about obedience which Christ called the sign of our love for Him (John 14:21), the man's response, "Which ones?" (v. 18), is telling. It indicates either his unwillingness to obey ALL the commandments or his hope that Jesus would give him an easy answer.

The love of God is central to the Ten Commandments about which we will elaborate in Chapter 7. Our love for God is demonstrated in our obedience to keeping these commandments. When we look at the Ten Commandments, the first four deal with our (vertical) relationship with God. The final six deal with our (horizontal) relationships with others. Jesus' response shows both his complete knowledge of the law and his complete understanding of this man's heart. Jesus lists five of the six "horizontal" commandments and sums them with the "second greatest commandment" (Matt. 22:39) of love your neighbor as yourself. One of the "horizontal" commandments is missing. Did Jesus forget? Hardly. The other commandment not listed is "Thou shall not covet" (Exodus 20:17). It is actually the tenth and final commandment. It is also the commandment with which this man struggled. It is this area of disobedience that represents the portion of the throne where this guy still clings, where he refuses lordship to Christ, where he refuses to mature and grow.

Now, back to where our chapter began – Matthew 5:48. This strange verse has troubled serious readers because of its apparent impossible connotations. However, when the meaning of perfect is seen in relation to the immediate context and in light of all we have discussed, much of the problem disappears. This verse cannot be divorced from the preceding section (vv. 43-47), in which the meaning of this perfection, the sign of our maturity, is spelled out, namely extending our love and goodwill toward those who persecute us. Sounds a lot like loving our neighbor as ourselves doesn't it? This pattern of love – revealed to us by Christ – is to become the norm, the standard for mature Christians. Being a mature Christian is not simply about right conduct, but more importantly about right attitudes. This characteristic of love is a quality, not an accomplishment.

Chapter 4

The Problem Of Self: Looking For God In The Mirror

―☯―

"God made man in His image, and ever since, man has been seeking to return the favor."

Voltaire

"Pride goes before destruction, a haughty spirit before a fall."

Proverbs 16:18

You were taught, with regard to your former way of life, to put off your old self, which is being corrupted by its deceitful desires; to be made new in the attitude of your minds; and to put on the new self, created to be like God in true righteousness and holiness.

Ephesians 4:22-24

I have always enjoyed the simplistic beauty found in the photography of Ansel Adams. Over the years more than a couple of his prints have been displayed in my home. He is best known for his stunning, scenic, black-and-white photographs of America's beautiful landscapes. One of his photographs is titled *"Mono Lake, Cloud Reflections"*. Mono Lake is located in California's spectacular Eastern Sierra and is an oasis in the dry Great Basin. The photograph captures the reflection of numerous billowing cumulus clouds in the glass-like surface of the lake; the waters are so calm that the reflection is nearly perfect. A perfect reflection requires a perfect surface.

After spending time in the last chapter expounding on Hebrews' definition of perfect, I feel obliged to briefly circle back and expound on the use of the word perfect in these previous two sentences. Without Christ, there is *nothing* you can do to become a perfect surface. It is He who perfects us, it is Christ who restores our relationship with God and in so doing affords us the ability to begin the process of continually and increasingly reflecting God. A relationship with God works to smooth the surface of your heart, preparing it for a perfect reflection of Him. However, there is only One who perfectly (completely) reflects God. Hebrews 1:3 states:

> The Son is the radiance of God's glory and the exact representation of his being, sustaining all things by his powerful word. After he had provided purification for sins, he sat down at the right hand of the Majesty in heaven. (Heb. 1:3-4)

Eugene Peterson paraphrases the above statement "The Son is the radiance of God's glory" stating "This Son perfectly mirrors God."[8] The calmness of the water in Ansel Adams' photograph is absolutely stunning. If the winds were blowing and the surface of the water was not so "perfect" the picture would not have the same impact. For Christians to become better reflections of God we need to calm the waters of our life. The author of Proverbs states:

> As water reflects a face, so a man's heart reflects the man. (Prov. 27:19)

My favorite scene in Disney's 1994 animated classic *The Lion King* provides a powerful illustration. It is the story of a lion, Simba, whose father, Mufasa, is the King of the Pride Lands. Mufasa's younger brother, Scar, desires the throne for himself and plots to kill both Mufasa and Simba. Scar's plot takes shape as his trio of hyena collaborators incites a stampede of wildebeest, putting Simba's life in jeopardy. Mufasa manages to save Simba but is betrayed and killed by Scar in the process. Scar then tricks Simba into believing that he was at fault for Mufasa's death. Feeling immense guilt and shame Simba flees the Pride Lands. Sometime later a now adult Simba is discovered by Rafiki his father's trusted aide who tries to convince Simba to return and reclaim his father's throne. However, Simba still believes that his father's death was his fault. Rafiki leads Simba to believe that his father is still alive, and he leads Simba to meet him. The journey takes Simba to a clearing with a small pond. As Simba steps forward to look

---

[8] Peterson, Eugene H.: *The Message: The Bible in Contemporary Language*. Colorado Springs, Colo. : NavPress, 2002, S. Heb 1:2-3

into the surface of the water he regrettably sees only his own reflection. Rafiki stirs the water with his finger and tells him to "look harder." As the disturbed surface of the water calms Simba's image transforms into that of his father, Mufasa. At that point Rafiki tells him, "You see, he lives in you!" It is then that Mufasa supernaturally appears in the clouds exhorting Simba saying, "Remember who you are!"

I am sure some of you are asking what do clouds and cartoon lions have to do with anything? Let's compare these reflections with others in the Bible. Who are some of the Biblical examples of those who "reflected" God? If you don't want to flip through all the pages in your Bible simply read the eleventh chapter of Hebrews. You will see names like Abel, Enoch, Noah, Abraham, Isaac, Jacob, Joseph, Moses, Rahab, Gideon, Barak, Samson, Jephthah, David and Samuel. Add to this list the Disciples, Paul, Timothy, Luke, James, Barnabas and the many other New Testament saints. Quite a list! If you read their individual stories, you begin to recognize that these people did not reflect God on their own; instead they were able to reflect God more and more as they allowed Him to flow through their lives.

When you look in the mirror who do you see? When others look at you who do they see? Why is it that so many Christians struggle to consistently reflect God? Why do we continually fail to align with Christ and cling to the throne of our hearts? There is a small word that has tripped up mankind, well, since the Garden of Eden. It is not vulgar, complex or difficult to pronounce. It is has one syllable, four letters, and it is only worth 7 points in Scrabble®: Self. What is the result when our love of self is greater than our love of God? What are the ramifications when we fail to shift the focus of our love from self to God? We are called to be lovers of God, but we are lured away by our other loves and fail to give our whole heart to Him. As Voltaire wrote, all too well, "God made man in His image, and ever since, man has been seeking to return the favor."

In what is widely believed to be his last letter, prior to his martyrdom, the Apostle Paul addressed this problem of self when he wrote his young friend and former travelling companion Timothy.

> But mark this: There will be terrible times in the last days. People will be lovers of themselves, lovers of money, boastful, proud, abusive, disobedient to their parents, ungrateful, unholy, without love, unforgiving, slanderous, without self-control, brutal, not lovers of the good, treacherous, rash, conceited, lovers of pleasure rather than lovers of God - having a form of godliness but denying its power. Have nothing to do with them. (2 Tim. 3:1-5)

In these verses, Paul lists a number of characteristics all linked to misdirected love that can become major road blocks to our Christ-directed maturation. Specifically, Paul shares three ways in which love becomes misdirected: Love of Self, Love of Money, and Love of Pleasure. When we cling to one of these loves we are clinging to the throne of our life. We must love God more than self, money, and pleasure!

We are created to love God. The problem is that our capacity to love God all too readily gets turned inward upon ourselves, bent towards money and inclined towards pleasure.

> "Love the Lord your God with all your heart and with all your soul and with all your mind. This is the first and greatest commandment. And the second is like it: 'Love your neighbor as yourself.'" (Matt. 22:37-39)

Jesus directs us to a love of self as the basis of a proper love of our neighbor: "love your neighbor as [you love] yourself." The love of self that is constructive is always tied to the love of others. When self-love becomes an end in itself, trouble begins. What would happen if we truly loved our neighbors as much as we love ourselves? Secondly, As with a healthy self-love, I believe there can be a healthy leveraging of money. Such love ties money to God and to others. Only when we regard money as a means of serving God and others, can we be liberated from its destructive power. What would happen if we worked to make money in order to give it away? Finally, in one sense we are very fortunate to live in a time and place where large numbers of people are able to participate in a lifestyle once only known by the wealthy and powerful. Billions of dollars are spent each year in America on leisure and recreational pursuits. The issue is *not* whether we should have pleasure but whether we should focus our affection upon pleasure. Pleasure has a way of possessing us. I have known individuals whose golf games and handicaps are more a root of anger and frustration than a source of enjoyment, relaxation and pleasure. If pleasure becomes the focus of our energy and resources, we are on a path where there is little room or energy for anything else. What would happen if our pursuit of pleasure was solely to establish a source of love for God and others?

Love not directed to God is, by definition, misdirected and is therefore, idolatry. Love of self, love of money, love of pleasure – rather than the love of God – is idolatry. As we have stated previously, becoming a Christian involves the spiritual, physical and mental turning from self to God. It is a transformative process where, as Paul states in 2 Corinthians, our faces increasingly mirror His glory.

> And we, who with unveiled faces all reflect the Lord's glory, are being transformed into his likeness with ever-increasing glory, which comes from the Lord, who is the Spirit. (2 Cor. 3:18)

Please note that the verse says "we are being transformed" not "we have been transformed". Our transformation is not complete (perfect). It goes on to say with *every increasing glory*.

Paul is saying that we are Christians if we are actively in the process of becoming more Christ-like. As Christ perfects the mirror of our lives, we reflect Him more and more.

In one of the most read chapters in the entire Bible, and one of the most popular readings at wedding ceremonies, Paul elaborately details this transformative love of God we are called to reflect. First Corinthians 13 is correctly titled the "love" chapter. You know it, "Love is patient, love is kind, it is not boastful etc. . ." Near the end of this beautiful chapter are these words:

> For we know in part and we prophesy in part, but when perfection comes, the imperfect disappears. When I was a child, I talked like a child, I thought like a child,
> I reasoned like a child. When I became a man, I put childish ways behind me. Now we see but a poor reflection as in a mirror; then we shall see face to face.
> Now I know in part; then I shall know fully, even as I am fully known. (1 Cor. 13:9-12)

I will be the first to admit how far short I fall of the perfect love that Christ models. However, these verses are another clear example of Christ's call for us to grow and mature into better reflections of His glory and love. In fact, translated perfection here is yet another use of the Greek word telos. It is a reference to God's call to completeness, maturity. There is nothing more important than allowing God to perfect His love in and through us. We are called to continue to learn and demonstrate love for others that mirrors His love for us. Love is the most important ingredient in the relationship between man and God.

Jesus gives us some very practical and real direction regarding this love. In the Gospel of John He says,

> My command is this: Love each other as I have loved you. Greater love has no one than this, that he lay down his life for his friends. You are my friends if you do what I command. (John 15:12-15)

And in the Gospel of Mark Jesus bluntly elaborates on this greater love.

> Then he called the crowd to him along with his disciples and said: "If anyone would come after me, he must deny himself and take up his cross and follow me. (Mark 8:34-35)

Unfortunately, many wrongly see the above verse as too burdensome. The words *deny* and *cross* have negative connotations. They see this call as totally unrealistic and either quit or don't even try. They see Christianity as boring and dull, a long list of chores, a bothersome lifestyle of burden. They see a trail of trial with no joy, no future.

Let's take a look at what Jesus is really saying when He shares these three significant commands: Deny yourself; Take up your cross; and Follow me. First, it would be a huge mistake to see self-denial as refusing pleasure or joy. In fact, one of the Pharisees' criticisms of Jesus was that He went to parties. On the contrary, we are called to deny many things that one would think we would readily desire to deny: jealousy, bitterness and anger. Think about those for a minute. When Jesus calls for us to ask for forgiveness to wash these destructive attitudes away, it is only our pride or self-pity that fights against seeking forgiveness. If we are honest with ourselves, we will admit this truth. It is our internal battle to deny these pressures to which Jesus is referring when He calls us to deny ourselves. When we are obedient and continue to deny ourselves of these poisons, we will find ourselves becoming more Christ-directed, more a reflection of who He is, and who He is calling us to become.

The second command is to take up our cross. First, notice that it is a call to take up *our* cross, not *His* Cross. Jesus' use of the imagery of the Cross is not to indicate that His command requires suffering – although it could. Instead the Cross represents His obedience to that which was God's will for Him. Our cross symbolizes our willingness to make daily choices of God's will for us—whatever that may prove to be. Willing obedience needs not be a burden. Jesus says "my yoke is easy" (Matt. 11:28-30). Instead of the above image of struggle and toil I have always cherished the imagery of the anonymous poem "Footprints". It is the image of a loving Savior who actually carries us when the burdens of life become overwhelming.

For years (yes I said years!) I have lifted the exact same requests to God in prayer. They included a personal area of ongoing temptation and spiritual struggle and the health of two loved ones who are not getting better. Over the years I have continued to struggle to understand why God has not answered these prayers the way I desire, and I want to know why God is still allowing certain temptations to be a thorn in my side. Did you notice how many times the word "I" is used in the above sentence? These frustrations were significantly hampering my ability to demonstrate Christ's love, be a better reflection of Him, in some of my most important relationships. A few weeks ago, while I was in the shower, I "heard" God say that the answer to my prayers is *no* (or at best wait . . . in faith . . . obediently) and that these requests, struggles, concerns are at this moment in my life, in fact, my cross. It became clear that I needed to carry this cross and follow Him. One thing I am learning is that it is very hard to grasp the throne of my life when I am faithfully carrying my cross.

This leads to the final command – Follow Me. This is not a command to trail after Him. This is not about trying to follow the tracks of some elusive, invisible quarry. It is the heart of Jesus' invitation to us. When Jesus says "Follow Me" he means walk with me. Go where I go. Do what I do. When we follow Jesus our aim should be to stay in step with His Spirit, the Holy Spirit. In fact, there is a wonderful name for the Holy Spirit in Greek. It is Paraclete which comes from two words.

"Para" means alongside (where we get the word parallel), and "clete" is to walk. Paraclete. Walk along side. How descriptive of God's desire for our relationship with Him. Only when we come alongside Jesus will we discover the strength we need daily to deny ourselves and carry our cross. And it is when our relationship with Christ is in step, in rhythm, resonating that we can lose that guilt and shame of our former self and its many failures. In denying ourselves, picking up our cross and following Jesus we begin to become not only what He calls us to be but what we have always desired to be.

Jesus is calling us to have a "bent" towards him not ourselves. We are called to an active spirit of yielding. It is this pursuit of yielding that is at the heart of Biblical perfection or spiritual maturity. There is no fence-riding here. Everyone is committed to something. It is out of these commitments, these inclinations that our actions arise and our character is defined. To what or to who are you inclined? What is your controlling center? We demonstrate our love for God, our inclination towards him, by denying self, picking up our cross and following Him. However, there is a small problem that I have failed to mention. In our humanness we are not naturally inclined to do any of these things. In fact, we are inclined to do exactly the opposite. And yielding or dedicating to any center outside of God (self, money, or pleasure) is sin, separation from God. As Paul correctly states,

> "I do not understand what I do. For what I want to do I do not do, but what I hate I do." (Rom. 7:15- 16)

Houston, we have a problem.

Chapter 5

The Problem Of Sin: "Houston, We Have A Problem"

"If 'sin' has become inflated in the secular world, its currency seems to have been devalued in Christian circles."

Anonymous

"One reason sin flourishes is that it is treated like a cream puff instead of a rattlesnake."

Billy Sunday

Who can say, "I have kept my heart pure; I am clean and without sin"?

Proverbs 20:9

It was my freshmen year in high school, Mr. Grey's biology class. I liked Mr. Grey but I will admit my first exposure to evolution in his class caught me ill prepared – but I digress. What I remember most from that class, is a question asked as part of the final exam. I also remember that it was worth 50 points – half of the overall total. It was a question that required an essay response: "What is life?"Is he serious? How does a high school freshman answer a question requiring knowledge of Chemistry and Physics - which I wouldn't even begin to have until my sophomore and junior years? How does a four-teen year old answer a question delving into the very depths of psychology and religion, when he can't drive a car? What is life? Does this sound like a strange question to you? Of course we all know what is meant by the word "life", but how would you define it? Even though we all seem to know what is meant by saying something is "alive", it's not very easy to describe what "life" is. It's almost as hard as describing where life came from.

 Here is another question. What is sin? Even though we all seem to know what is meant by saying someone is a "sinner", it's not very easy to describe what "sin" is. It is almost as hard as describing where sin came from. Let me see if I can answer the former while not getting mired in the latter. I know what you are thinking. Come on Jon! What is the big deal with sin? Didn't you say in the last chapter that "self" is the small word that has tripped up mankind? Yes I did. But, if we peel back one more layer we see why self is such a problem. At its heart is this even smaller word of only three letters that is the source of more theological debate and documentation than any other topic, sin.

According to Webster, sin is a fault, error, a violation of a moral law. On the surface this appears to be a straight forward answer. But dig deeper and you discover just how complex this question becomes and how far short this simple answer falls. To put this challenge in perspective I referenced one of my Bible dictionaries. Look up sin and you will find a whopping 16 pages dedicated to the definition! Now that will make your brain hurt. Look up the word "love" and you will over 20 pages. Seems like an awful lot of writing about two one syllable words. I trust the fact that there are more pages about love than sin is a good thing . . . I think. Here is what I do know. Both of these words are non-trivial. They are the root of the problem and the solution. We will be getting to the solution a bit later. For now, however, it is very important that Christians, all Christians, grasp what sin is and how pervasively destructive it is to all of creation.

As I mentioned in the introduction I am not a theologian, nor am I a Pastor. My degrees are in Aerospace Engineering. I have always been fascinated with satellites, rockets and space travel. It probably comes as no surprise that one of my favorite movies is Apollo 13. Watching the flight director, Gene Kranz, lead the ground team's discovery of a solution for a seemingly hopeless situation is an ultimate example of engineering. During the movie Astronaut James Lovell says one of the greatest understatements of all time, "Houston, we have a problem." Similarly, any trite treatise on sin would be an understatement on a universal level. If we fail to acknowledge sin, we fail to appreciate the cross. If we fail to understand sin we fail to grasp the infinite extent of God's love.

So, what is sin? In his first epistle John (1 John 3:4) simply states that sin is lawlessness. Great! So what is lawlessness? It doesn't take long to understand why there are 16 pages of definition for this word in my Bible dictionary. With that said I can safely guarantee that most theologians will find some-

The Problem Of Sin: "Houston, We Have A Problem"

thing in this discussion with which they will disagree. That is okay. I mean, simply Google the word sin and you will get over 1.2 *billion* (with a B!) responses. Incredible! Random clicks on just a few of these responses and I quickly find myself immersed in theological papers detailing such terms as depravity, original sin, habituation, and non-conformity. I discovered strong (in some cases flat out nasty) debates on topics such as imputed versus imparted, human versus carnal nature, and moral versus substantive. Well, rest assured this chapter will not descend (too far) into the academic and theological debate called hamartiology: the study of sin.

Beyond the obvious fact that sin is a real problem it has become a politically incorrect topic to discuss - even in many churches. It's almost as if talking about sin *is* a sin. Yet, if you want to know why there are so many Christian denominations it is usually the consequence of either which musical instruments are allowed on the platform or differences of opinion when defining this small word. For instance, compare the accepted definitions for "original sin" by Roman Catholics, Lutherans, Anglicans, Presbyterians, Methodists and Baptists and you will see there is not one single, agreed upon definition. I have talked to a number of very smart people about sin; teachers, preachers and theologians. I have read more than a few books and articles on the topic. Most talk about the various "dimensions" or "definitions" or "aspects" of sin. Some say there is one "dimension", while most say two, three or four "dimensions". And of course they rarely agree on those "dimensions". Some will say that others' views are too narrow. Still others argue that the opposing opinions are talking about "things" that are not really sins but simply "mistakes", "faults" or "errors".

However, at the core there is a very black and white area of agreement. It should not be surprising that the further you move away from this core area of agreement, the more theological the discussion becomes, the grayer the agreement becomes and the more heated the debate. I am not so naïve as to fail to recognize that the following paragraphs may exasperate or vex some of you who are a bit more "studied". My goal is not to solve the universal debate about sin, but I hope to challenge all of you to truly ponder the concept of sin, its impacts on your life, and our desperate need for God's grace. I am convinced that an honest journey of discovery on this topic can open your eyes, then your mind and hopefully your heart to the tremendous impact sin has on our view of God, our relationship with Him and the victorious life to which He calls. It has been for me. We cannot truly appreciate God's love for us and the grace He so freely extends unless we fully grasp the predicament in which we all find ourselves.

Let's first differentiate "sins" from "sin". Jesus said, "I tell you the truth, everyone who sins is a slave to sin" (John 8:34) While "sins" are what we are all traditionally comfortable defining, "sin" is really the condition that leads to "sinning". Confused yet? If so, please bear with me. To keep this manageable let's start with "sin". Sin is spiritual. It is a relational term. It is not a physical "thing". If sin is relational with whom is it relating? Obviously not God, but to say Satan would be too simple an answer . . . and incorrect.

I remember watching a movie back in the 80s which was not what I would now call family friendly. The main character, in the midst of his attempt at a motivational speech states, "There's something wrong with us! Something very, very wrong with us! Something seriously wrong with us!" He was right. It is called sin. While theologians apparently enjoy debating the origin of sin, and even more importantly how did this "original sin" become ours today, I find it, to some extent, analogous to the chicken and the egg conundrum. Which came first the chicken or the egg? Those debates are great academic theater but for me it is quite simple. It doesn't matter. I know there are chickens and I know there are eggs. We don't have eggs without chickens and we don't have chickens without eggs. What I am very sure of is that both chickens and eggs exist.

This is what I do know. Adam (and Eve) sinned. Something happened. Adam and Eve were created "good". Enabled by the presence of God they were "right" in his sight. They were righteous. We were created in the image of God (Gen. 1:27), but their failure in the Garden of Eden resulted in this separation from God. As a result we have become corrupted, damaged. Something broke. Sin is not simply a tumor that can be permanently (this side of Heaven) extracted. Sin is a condition. It is a break in our relationship with God that has resulted in an all permeating corruption of the original creation of God which He called "good" (Gen. 1:31). God's good creation was damaged, it remains damaged, and as a result I am damaged. We became deprived of the relational presence of God that made us "right". I am not going to say I fully understand this because I don't. What I know is that this sin condition, this broken relationship, this separation from God is real and has totally corrupted the present state in which we live. Regardless of how we got to this realization, we are here. Sin is a current condition, a reality we cannot totally escape, which has resulted in an irreconcilable separation from the indwelling presence of God. It started when Adam and Eve were expelled from the Garden (Gen. 3:23-24) and continues today. God is holy. We are not. In case you are not taking notes this is a real problem.

While we are still created in the image of God, we are now also in Adam's image – our own image, our "self". Alienation deprives us of the sanctifying relationship with the Creator, resulting in total depravity. We have become like a branch cut from the vine; damaged not by the addition of something but by the loss of something. Jesus says it Himself:

> If anyone does not remain in me, he is like a branch that is thrown away and withers; such branches are picked up, thrown into the fire and burned. (John 15:6-7)

Separation from God deprives us of His spiritual life and without some outside intervention, will eventually result in spiritual death. So, where does this intervention originate?

Not with us. We are incapable of bridging this chasm of sin. On our own we will forever remain separated. The problem of self (disobedience, self-sovereignty) brought initial alienation from God and expulsion from the Garden. Our own self-centeredness still results in this same alienation today.

Do not underestimate the destructive, depriving power of this separation nor the resulting depravity in which we exist. We are so totally corrupt that we are free to do little more than live lives focused entirely on ourselves. In its totality, infinite separation from God's sanctifying presence, our state of total depravity and the complete inability on our own to bridge this chasm called sin, removes even the desire to try to address our own hopelessness. Sounds pretty gloomy I know. It should. However, let's be clear on one more point. This state of total depravity does not mean that we are as thoroughly corrupt in our actions ("sins") as we possibly could be. It does not mean that everyone indulges in every form of sin, nor does it mean that people cannot perform acts of kindness and goodness. I would hope that your own Christian experiences would agree to this understanding. When we use the word total we mean that the effects and consequences of this condition extend to everyone. It is universal.

Do you struggle with this concept of complete and total depravity which results from our separation of the sanctifying presence of God? The Bible is very clear on this point. Paul states it this very succinctly,

> For all have sinned and fall short of the glory of God. (Rom. 3:23)

If this is not black and white enough, simply look at Paul's preceding verses where he states:

> There is no one righteous, not even one (v10)
> There is no one who understands, no one who seeks God (v11)
> All have turned away (v12)

When Paul says all have sinned he means ALL have sinned. We have fallen prey to our own deprivation. We are sinners. We are ALL damaged, corrupted, and guilty. If you are still struggling with this horrible reality, I would warn you not to read the Apostle John's thoughts on the subject. In his first epistle he states:

> If we claim to be without sin, we deceive ourselves and the truth is not in us. If we confess our sins, he is faithful and just and will forgive us our sins and purify us from all unrighteousness. If we claim we have not sinned, we make him out to be a liar and his word has no place in our lives. (1 John 1:8- 10)

The whole of creation is out of joint. Broken. At its core, sin is the rupture in the relationship between creation and the Creator.

As I mentioned earlier, sin is a relational term. Actually it is an absence of relationship with God. When we are deprived of the indwelling presence of God, for which we were created, we struggle; searching for poor and inadequate substitutes. We can all name the standard substitutes: money, fame, family, work, drugs, food, immorality, the list goes on and on. All are rooted in our own selfishness. We have put self on the throne of our hearts instead of God, loving ourselves instead of Him. In this light, sin can be simply defined as *perverted love*. God is love, and God is holy. Man is sinful.

Paul repeatedly tackles this discussion of sin/sinner/self. On four occasions in the King James Version (KJV) he uses the expressions "old man" and "new man", namely, Romans 6:6; Ephesians 2:15; 4:22-24; and Colossians 3:9-11. Other translations replace "man" with "self" ("old self" and "new self"). In Chapter 8 I will be talking about moving from "in Adam" to "in Christ"; from our "old man" to our "new man" so I won't belabor that quite yet. Put simply the "old man" refers to people in solidarity with Adam under the old age of sin, death, and judgment. It is the condition where humanity has been separated from God. Similarly, the new man is synonymous with the church, the Body of Christ. Finally, through Christ's sacrifice on the Cross, Christians have been completely and decisively brought back into relationship with our loving Father. However, we still have the tendency to be drawn back into the "old" relationship with Adam. We live in the "now" but also the "not-yet". This tension will remain until God glorifies those he justifies (Romans 8:30).

This is a good place to transition from "sin", the "old man" to "sins". Sin is evident from birth. It is not something we learn. Being separated and depraved appears very early in the lives of every child. Words like "no" and "mine" are universal in a two year old. Do you need to teach a child to be selfish or do you teach them to share? Every parent knows the answer to that question. Now while some Christian traditions hold infants responsible for these actions, and the condition into which they are born, other traditions do not. Based on what I have read in Scripture I resonate with the latter view. Again, I don't presuppose to grasp the mysteries of God's grace, love and holiness. But I do trust Him.

I am not prepared or qualified (no one truly is) to expound on this mystery – so I won't. However, I can talk about those areas where the Bible is explicit about our responsibilities. Let me ask you something. For those we would all agree are lost – the unrepentant murderer or child molester – do you think God is more concerned with their "sins" or their "sin"? How is this question for a debate starter? Two of the most memorized scriptures in the Bible I believe give the answer.

> For it is by grace you have been saved, through faith-and this not from yourselves, it is the gift of God - not by works, so that no one can boast. (Eph. 2:8-10)

> For God so loved the world that he gave his one and only Son, that whoever believes in him shall not perish but have eternal life. For God did not send his Son into the world to condemn the world, but to save the world through him. Whoever believes in him is not condemned, but whoever does not believe stands condemned already because he has not believed in the name of God's one and only Son.[9] (John 3:16-18)

It is my belief that God's first concern is our "sin", our condition, our separation. If the separation is not addressed how can His healing begin? As the Church we spend too much time pointing fingers at how the lost are dressed or act or smell. We take issue with their choices in music, their language and their habits. We would be well served to take a long look in the mirror and grasp the truth - that God loves the lost as much as He loves us. We deserve His grace no more than those we dare call the "worst" sinners.

Forgive me as I put down my pen and step on my soapbox for a moment to talk straight to those of you that would say you are a Christian. Depravity is alive and well in our churches today. We have Christians addicted to pornography. Church leaders embezzling money. Pastors molesting children. We have regular attenders being fired from their jobs for racial emails. I have heard Christian parents expressing their discomfort with the fact that their child is being exposed to too much ethnic diversity in their grade school. I have even heard one family express disappointment in their pastor for what they viewed as favoritism to another mother's child whose young father tragically died. Look at this list and tell me that depravity is not total. You have probably heard the saying that when you point your finger at someone, three fingers are pointing back at you. Our concern should not be limited solely to the sin all around us, but within us. When you are tempted to point out the flaws of others, remember that you are really only pointing out the things that are equally true of you. Sin is sin. We are lost. We are depraved.

An Old Testament story of King David comes to mind. Instead of being out with his troops in battle, he is in his palace, peeping at the beautiful Bathsheba as she is bathing on a nearby rooftop. This man, after God's own heart (1 Samuel 13:14, Acts 13:22) commences in making his sexual desires more important than his relationship to God. He covets his neighbor's wife, steals her, commits adultery and then proceeds to lie and eventually commits murder in an attempt to cover his tracks. As the story unfolds, David violates SIX of the Ten Commandments. Enter the prophet Nathan, who tells the King a story about two men, one wealthy and one poor. He describes the large flock of sheep available to the rich man, but also the single lamb that the poor man owned and loved. When a meal was required for a guest in the home of the rich man, instead of selecting one of the many sheep in his own flock, he used his position of power to take the beloved lamb of the poor man, had it slaughtered and prepared for his visitor. David predictably responds in anger, saying the rich man, while deserving death must also pay substantial reparations. It is then that Nathan reveals to David the cold, hard truth, "You are the man!" We are spiritually and morally responsible beings. No amount of denial or finger pointing can change this fact, for this reason, Paul says,

> "You, therefore, have no excuse, you who pass judgment on someone else, for at whatever point you judge the other, you are condemning yourself, because you who pass judgment do the same things. (Rom. 2:1)

We will all be held accountable before God for what we know. The ultimate day of accountability will come when God finally judges men. Thankfully, God has offered grace through His son Jesus Christ and the Cross.

The Problem Of Sin: "Houston, We Have A Problem"

Years ago the WWJD (What Would Jesus Do) bracelets were the fad. It was a great reminder of the life that Christians are called to live. We are to live every moment in a fashion that is Christ-like. As we have previously discussed we cannot live perfectly this side of heaven. Accepting Christ does not divorce us from our "self". It is only a lifelong relationship with Him, obedience to Him and life in Him that enables us to progressively become more and more Christ-like. This relationship, this walking with Christ is full of daily choices, daily conversations and daily opportunities to choose actions in accordance with WWJD.

Now some (maybe many) will have a hard time with this next statement, but I believe that whenever we fail to act Christ-like we sin. James states it plainly,

> Anyone, then, who knows the good he ought to do and doesn't do it, sins. (James 4:17)

Please don't rush to extremes thinking that since Jesus never married that I believe marriage is a sin or that asparagus must be off the menu if Jesus (hypothetically) didn't like the vegetable. Let's keep our eye on the ball here. We are talking about those thoughts and actions, in word or deed, that in our heart as Christians we know are not Christ-like. I am not going to get into a discussion of semantics where some acts are sins and others are errors of judgment or mistakes. Child molestation, cheating on your taxes, racially demeaning statements about those God loves or gossiping about your neighbor are not mistakes. When we act this way we miss the mark of Christ-likeness. We sin. Another way of stating this is that anything short of perfect (complete) holiness is sin.

The next obvious rebuttal to this line of thinking is how could we ever live a life totally free from sinning? Well, I don't think we can. Yes, we can accept the gift of grace that makes us "right" in God's sight. We can connect with the indwelling, sanctifying power of Christ. This addresses the state of sin – our condition of being separated from God. However, we still live in a world that is totally depraved. Satan is still lurking waiting to devour us (1 Peter 5:8). While God's gift of grace begins to heal the damage of our depravity, it is only as we walk in this light that we can hope to have the strength to be obedient (WWJD). I believe it is unrealistic to expect totally sinless lives but we should strive towards this end.

I am NOT condoning sin nor abandoning ourselves to a life of sinfulness. What I am saying is that God's call for our perfection is our willingness to walk with Him, but when we fall, ask forgiveness and try again. God is ready and willing to support us:

> For the eyes of the Lord range throughout the earth to strengthen those whose hearts are fully committed to him. (2 Chron. 16:9)

Two of my personal challenges along my journey have been to more clearly grasp just what exactly God desires from me as a Christian, and to rely more on His grace than my capabilities. Somewhere, the notions that not only can my sinful nature be eradicated but so can sinning itself. These notions had insidiously warped my view of His grace. This distortion of grace was hindering my ability to translate my faith head knowledge to heart action. I had been taught that by faith, when I accept Christ as my Savior, my sins are forgiven and the state of separation from God has been reconciled. I understood that I was justified and made righteous by the grace of God. I believed that the sanctifying power of God began to work in my life, healing the damage, cleansing the depravity. And this is an ongoing walk of dependency upon God for the rest of my earthly life.

This notion that I can live here on earth without sinning has not, and does not hold up against my experience, nor does it hold up against what I have read in the New Testament. The danger of believing in some mystical event where God extracts the "seed" of our sinful nature has been conveyed as the means whereby we can live without sinning. Some have gone on to equate this sinlessness with Christian perfection. It is no wonder so many find "perfection" to be impossible. It is my opinion that this line of logic requires a very narrow view of sin, which is a dangerous path to self-justification of what are sins and what are errors, faults or mistakes. The real question is not if perfection is too high of a standard, but if we are defining sin in so small of a way that the idea of perfection becomes irrelevant. Likewise we must not fall into the trap that sin is a "thing" that is simply removed by God. Just think about what that would mean. If God simply removed some "thing" that equated with our sin, what would be left of any moral responsibility on our part? This line of logic is not Biblical. We need to be careful not to simply look for some way to escape personal responsibility for being what we are, and fail to recognize our continual need to confess our sins to our Savior. Our problem is not some alien "thing" clinging to our soul but our own alienation from God. Our problem is not the semantics of sin but separation. Let's never forget that.

But there is good news! Thanks be to God (Romans 7:25) that we have a Savior. I would be totally irresponsible to simply define sin without addressing adequately our means of escape. I will discuss this in greater detail in Chapter 8, but for now know that our righteousness is sustained in our ongoing relationship with God. Holiness consists of this unobstructed personal communion and deep, personal fellowship with God. Sin is simply the absence of this relationship because we have rejected God's free gift of grace through Jesus Christ our Lord. Pardon the repetition but let me state it one last time. We have two problems - we were born in "sin" and we commit "sins". But Christ has defeated both for us. Let's look at three passages of Scripture as a means to transition to the remainder of this book. First in Ephesians Paul states:

> In him we have redemption through his blood, the forgiveness of sins, in accordance with the riches of God's grace that he lavished on us with all wisdom and understanding. (Eph. 1:7-8)

Please note the tense. Jesus has forgiven our sins – the things we do. We have redemption. We have forgiveness. It is a present possession of the Christian! Second, let's look at the landmark first four verses of Romans 8:

> Therefore, there is now no condemnation for those who are in Christ Jesus, because through Christ Jesus the law of the Spirit of life set me free from the law of sin and death. For what the law was powerless to do in that it was weakened by the sinful nature, God did by sending his own Son in the likeness of sinful man to be a sin offering. And so he condemned sin in sinful man, in order that the righteous requirements of the law might be fully met in us, who do not live according to the sinful nature but according to the Spirit. (Rom. 8:1-4)

Jesus has condemned "sin" – separation from God. He defeated it at the Cross. The Cross forever acts as our bridge to a relationship with God.

Part II:

The Path of Promise

Discovering How to Click with God

Chapter 6

Putting First Things First
The Clickability Factor

'To fall in love with God is the greatest of all romances; to seek Him, the greatest adventure; to find him, the greatest human achievement."

Augustine

I love those who love me, and those who seek me find me.

Proverbs 8:17

I was upside down, dangling over 100 feet above the rocky slope below. The living canvas of the Rocky Mountains was laid bare around me with its breathtaking grandeur, but I was a bit too preoccupied to truly enjoy the view. The day had started just like the one before, I was part of a group of teenagers who awoke in a rustic cabin at Young Life's Frontier Ranch, located about 120 miles southwest of Denver. Today was rappelling day, and we were all excited, confident, and a bit naive. Following breakfast, our group hiked up the slopes of Mt. Princeton whose peak towered over 14,000 feet next to our camp. Expectations soared as we made our way up the trail, completely unaware of the true challenge ahead. We arrived at a small plateau. A wooden platform cantilevered over the edge of a near 120 foot cliff. Fifty teenagers, two rappelling instructors, fifteen minutes of *Rappelling 101* and no fatalities -God is amazing! However, my initial foray into rappelling was not.

Rappelling requires rope, a safety helmet, a harness, carabineers, and most importantly something called a rappel device. Rappel devices come in countless shapes and sizes. Their sole purpose is to create friction, allowing rope to be paid out in a controlled fashion and with minimal effort. The speed at which the person is rappelled is controlled by applying greater or lesser friction to the rope. Rappelling is not belaying. Belaying is what we all see at a commercial climbing wall, which includes a second person on the ground (the belayer) who controls the amount and speed at which the rope is released. When you rappel, you must trust the equipment. The rappel device controls the rope and the speed, the harness holds the rappeller, and the carabineer attaches the rappel device to the harness. Without the carabineer the best rope, helmets and rappel devices in the world won't do much good. So how does the carabineer do its job? Carabineers are simply big, strong clips. You slide the harness loop and one end of the rappel device onto the carabineer and then you *click* the carabineer closed. Do not forget to *click*. If you fail to *click* you will render the best tools in the world useless. Get the picture?

Equipped and clicked I was instructed to back up to the edge of the cliff, put my trust in the equipment, lean back until my body was perpendicular to the cliff face and simply walk backwards down the cliff. Oh, and don't look down! Did I mention it was a 120 foot high sheer cliff? It suddenly became clear why my parents' had to sign a waiver of liability! Talk about a great lesson in trust. I took a few awkward steps, looked down (oops) and froze. This would not have been a problem, but in my panic I forgot to fully engage the rappel device resulting in too much slack in the rope. In the blink of an eye I was upside down. Thank goodness, at this moment the rappel device automatically went to work and safely held me tight. After some simple words of encouragement from the instructor some 20 feet above me I was able to right myself and rappel to the bottom intact, with only my ego was slightly bruised.

Let me tell you what I learned on that day nearly 30 years ago. To rappel you must learn to trust. Trust your rope. Trust the rappel device. But most importantly, you must trust the click of the carabineer. Rappelling is easy and fun once you learn to commit and have faith in the equipment. It takes a leap of faith to move from being told the equipment will hold you safely to actually walking backwards off that 120 foot cliff. However, once you trust, and step off the edge, you experience the wonder of rappelling. What is true in rappelling is true in our spiritual lives. It is this *clicking* that connects us with the very tools designed for our effective Christian walk. To click is to engage, when we say something *clicks* - it feels right, it fits.

I have worked in the secular world for over 20 years. Throughout my career, I have interviewed and hired a wide variety of individuals. When I first started interviewing for positions, I was not very successful, and unfortunately I made some poor hiring decisions. I did not know the best questions to ask, how to recognize who would be best suited to succeed, and how to ensure that myself, the company and the new hire would find success in the relationship. Time and experience has given me some good insights into a process that now works well for me. Although simple, at its heart is the test for "clickability". Every open position would result in numerous resumes and applications. I would quickly filter these using a variety of details that I will not belabor here and once I had a short list I would setup a time to casually meet the various applicants over coffee. This was not a formal interview. We would just talk. My goal was to discover if we clicked personally, if we clicked professionally, and if I thought the candidate would click within our organization and its culture. I have discovered that having this feeling of clickability is critical to a successful relationship. Once I sensed clickability I would arrange the formal interviews to ensure a fit professionally and technically.

But let's be clear on some semantics - clicking is not cliquing. Clicking is exceptional. Cliquing tends to be exclusionary. Clicking connects. Cliquing divides. Clicking is not cliquing. Our lives, our churches, our faith should be clicking not cliquey. As Christians we are called to click with our communities. The Church must be where people can come, as they are, and discover they are loved. We must be about the business of the Great Commission in our homes, in our churches, in our workplaces and in our communities. Are we engaging others in a meaningful way with the Gospel? Are we clicking? We must trust God and learn to click. We must learn to click with God and we must learn to click with others.

Can I let you in on a little secret? I have often struggled to know that I am clicking with God. This book is really the result of a personal journey to (re)discover truths I too often forget. It is about discovering and knowing that we are clicking with God, and why that matters. Over the years there have been times when I know I was clicking with God. I was where God wanted me to be, doing what God asked me to do. Other times it has been much less clear. As I write this book I find myself backing up to the edge of that cliff in Colorado, remembering what it means to trust God and the equipment he has given me, to click. One common question I am asked on this topic is if clicking is related to reaching our goals. Let me answer with an illustration.

John Goddard is best known for his so called "Life List"[10]. At the age of 15 John listed 127 things he wanted to accomplish in his lifetime. According to his website, as of publication, he has checked off an amazing 110 of those 127 goals. The 17 he has not completed includes being in a Tarzan movie, visiting both the North and South poles, and landing on the moon. Among the goals he has achieved are such things as learning French, Spanish and Arabic, and visiting all but 30 countries in the world as visiting every country is one of his goals. While John Goddard's achievements are nothing short of extraordinary, achieving our goals, no matter how lofty, still falls far short of clicking with God.

In his short essay, Tyranny of the Urgent, Charles E. Hummel quotes an experienced cotton mill manager who once said, "Your greatest danger is letting the urgent things crowd out the important."[11] What he is saying is that there exists a constant tension between what is truly important and only urgent. As Christians we desperately need to focus on the best, even when it is at the expense of the good. We too often fail to love God through our time in the Word, prayer, worship and service. We fail to love our neighbor when we

---

[10] http://www.johngoddard.info/life_list.htm

[11] Charles E. Hummel, *Tyranny of the Urgent*, 196, *Intervarsity Christian Fellowship, Downers Grove, Il 60515*

don't find time to show compassion, lend a helping hand or a witness (verbal or silent). All of these best things fall to the wayside as we are buried under the urgent things such as email, telemarketers, television and the internet. However, even if we are able to maximize time on those things that are truly important and minimize the time spent on the trivial, we are still only doing what we believe to be best. This type of goal setting and prioritization still falls short of clicking. As a matter of fact it can make clicking much more complicated than it needs to be.

Clicking is simply connecting to God's one thing for your life. And I know your next question – then what is that one thing? How many of you remember the 1991 movie, City Slickers? It is the story of a man, Mitch, played by Billy Crystal, who is going through a midlife crisis. He, along with two of his fellow midlife crisis friends go on a two week cattle drive. One of the most quoted dialogs in the movie takes place between Mitch and a tough as nails trail boss named Curly played by Jack Palance. As they are off on their own tracking down strays Curly asks Mitch if knows what the secret of life is. Mitch says no and Curly responds by holding up a single finger saying that the secret of life is one thing. Just one thing. Intrigued, Mitch wants to know what the one thing is, but Curly says that Mitch must discover that for himself. Let's go on our own journey to discover this one thing for each of our lives. So the main thing is then to discover God's one thing for our lives, and then to keep the one thing the main thing. Goals and priorities are not the one thing – they are the details. Priorities are plural, the one thing is singular. Priorities are dynamic. They change from year to year (do you remember your New Year's resolutions?); they often change moment to moment. This is true because we are temporal beings. We cannot be in two places at once, much less the ten that are seemingly required some days. Because of this we are constantly faced with choices that call us to decide what is best – most important – in that moment.

There are times (moments) when our family requires our full attention; to be our top priority. This means that in those moments they have priority over your church board meetings, over your job, even your golf league. However, in other specific moments your family may not be the top priority. You are called to the hospital after a dear friend is in a terrible car accident. In those moments it does NOT mean that your family is not important. It means in those moments they may not be most important. However, the one thing does NOT change. Whether we are with our family, at the hospital with a friend or at golf league the one thing remains the one thing. What we will discover is that God calls us as Christians to decide what is most important in the moments based on our daily living of this one thing. So, what is this one thing, already? I am glad you asked! Let me give you three Scriptural examples of David's, Paul's and Christ's one thing. And surprise – they are all the same!

Chapter 7

Choices, Choices, Choices: Life's Proverbial Forks In The Road

---

When you have to make a choice and don't make it, that is in itself a choice.

William James

Life is the sum of all your choices.

Albert Camus

But if serving the Lord seems undesirable to you, then choose for yourselves this day whom you will serve, whether the gods your forefathers served beyond the River, or the gods of the Amorites, in whose land you are living. But as for me and my household, we will serve the Lord.

Joshua 24:15

We all have choices, endless choices in our everyday lives. Most are trivial (or if you want a fancier word – pedantic). Which socks to wear? Should I eat breakfast? Which route should I take to work? Every day the list seems endless. Some choices are instructive or didactic, while other choices can have significant moral connotations. Let's focus on the latter for our purposes. This chapter will not be a debate about whether Robert Frost's traveler took the road less traveled because he was a puppet directed by the strings of unperceived powers or whether he freely chose the path "that made all the difference". Instead let's focus on the reality that life is a series of choices, some trivial, some spiritually critical.

Right or wrong - where does my moral compass point? Which path *should* I take? Which path *do* I take? The Christian walk is a series of unending moral decisions. His will or ours? His *way* or ours? Sometimes these choices are black and white, but we all know that some fall into a grey area. When discussing the topic of choices I have always sketched on a whiteboard a simple fork in the road with a large C (for choice) standing firmly at the point of decision. Why does life present us with so many of these proverbial forks in the road? For that matter why does God create rules for us to follow? Are these rules absolute? Are there any grey areas? Is there any room for negotiation? Let's start with the question "why are there rules?"

In the Bible rules are often called commandments or laws. I would assume most people could name at least some of the Ten Commandments (see Exodus 20 if you need some help). But there are a lot more than the Ten Commandments in the Bible. In fact there are (by most counts) 613 rabbinical laws in the Old Testament, of which 247 are found in the Book of Leviticus alone. That is a lot of laws and regulations. As a side note, there are many commandments that people believe are in the Bible, but actually are not.

Do any of these sound familiar?

Do unto others as you would have them do unto you.
God helps those who help themselves.
Money is the root of all evil.
Cleanliness is next to godliness.
Pride comes before the fall.

None of the above is actually found in the Bible. However, many of the 613 laws, commandments and rules that are found relate to sacrificial, ceremonial, civil and judicial codes, meant to maintain the moral purity of Israel. So, are all of these 613 laws still relevant? More importantly, are they absolute? Many, I am sure, cringe at the mere notion that they are not, but rest assured I am not making that statement (yet).

So why are there so many rules? In short, God gave us commandments not to necessitate choices, but rather to help guide His people to make Godly choices. Because of the commandments we have been made aware of the right choices (Romans 7). The question is then, how do we filter through and find the guideposts in these laws. Which ones, if any, are greater than others? What should be our "one thing"? Let me present three Scriptural examples of David, Paul and Christ's one thing.

In Psalm 27 David gives us a single-minded confession of trust and faith. In verse four he writes:

> One thing I ask of the Lord, this is what I seek: that I may dwell in the house of the Lord all the days of my life, to gaze upon the beauty of the Lord and to seek him in his temple. (Ps. 27:4)

David's desire is to live where God is and to spend his life in His presence. Please note the sequence of David's request. First, to dwell with the Lord, second, to gaze upon His beauty (referring to David's desire to worship God), lastly, David seeks God. Here seeking is really about opening our hearts to God. David's one thing is not just to go to church, but rather it is to live in fellowship with an ever present God.

Now fast forward approximately 1000 years to the New Testament and the Apostle Paul. In his letter to the Philippians Paul offers the following open and honest confession:

> I want to know Christ and the power of his resurrection and the fellowship of sharing in his sufferings, becoming like him in his death, and so, somehow, to attain to the resurrection from the dead. (Phil. 3:10-11)

For years this passage has been my life verses. These two verses represent my ultimate spiritual goal, my top priority, and my one thing. This testimony was meant to remind the believers at Philippi – and us today – that spiritual growth is not a goal to be achieved, but rather a journey with our Savior. It is not as if we can say today "I am fully spiritually grown" (mature or perfect). We must remain continually in the process of growing. While there is enough meat in these verses for multiple sermons I want to spend a few moments paying close attention to what Paul is saying in two phrases.

The first phrase I want to focus on is "I want to know Christ" (v. 10). Paul uses the word *gnōnai* which means "to know by experience." This is how Paul wanted to know Christ. Knowing something in your head is very different than experiencing it and *knowing* it in your heart. Paul then adds "becoming like him" (v. 10) which translates to *symmorphizomenos*, meaning "being conformed inwardly in one's experience to something." There is that word experience again. It is important to not lose sight of the fact that Paul is not saying he had accomplished either of these statements. Rather his one thing is to continually accomplish them – yesterday, today and tomorrow. Paul is affirming that he had not yet attained these goals. Rather, he was pressing on "toward the goal to win the prize" (v. 14). Do you see the difference? Paul had good goals, but his one thing was *how* he wanted to achieve them.

So, we have seen what David and Paul consider their "one thing". In both cases they desired "to know" God, and by knowing God they could know how to maneuver the daily minefields of choices and decisions. What did Jesus say on this topic? Let's take a look at the events beginning the last week before His crucifixion. The scene is described in the 21st and 22nd chapters of Matthew's Gospel (see also Mark 11-12). It begins on Palm Sunday. Everything Jesus did during his earthly ministry was done for a purpose. Most Christians have distinct images of Palm Sunday engraved in their minds; Jesus riding a donkey up to Jerusalem, people lining the path with palm branches cheering His arrival. Yet we all know that by the end of that very week, Jesus was crucified. Of course, Jesus knew that too, His entry was but one purposeful element of His larger mission in Jerusalem. It included the subsequent cleansing of the Temple, and His challenges to both the Pharisees and Sadducees. He cursed the fig tree to illustrate judgment upon fruitlessness, and a trilogy of parables regarding His authority.

It is following this trilogy of parables that Jesus entertains questions from the conniving leaders trying to trap him with His answers. However, the result is a wonderful description of Jesus' one thing for our lives. First the Pharisees attempt to trick Jesus with a question about whether or not taxes should be paid to Caesar. Completely confounded by the wisdom of Jesus' answer, the scene takes on the feel of something along the lines of a tag team wrestling match. While Jesus calmly remains in the ring, the Pharisees, desperately needing to regroup, tag in none other than their heated enemies the Sadducees who then leap into the ring with questions about the resurrection. They too are amazed at Jesus' words and are forced to tap out. Reenergized and (for some reason) over confident, the Pharisees retag for round two and have one of their own – a lawyer – set what they believe is the final trap:

> Hearing that Jesus had silenced the Sadducees, the Pharisees got together. One of them, an expert in the law, tested him with this question: "Teacher, which is the greatest commandment in the Law?" (Matt. 22:34-36)

Oh the humanity! There are 613 laws. What an unfair question. If it had not been so sad to see the "religious leaders" behave so blindly, I think Jesus would have smirked. Instead He simply replied:

> 'Love the Lord your God with all your heart and with all your soul and with all your mind.' This is the first and greatest commandment. And the second is like it: 'Love your neighbor as yourself.' All the Law and the Prophets hang on these two commandments." (Matt. 22:37-40)

Oh, that was easier than I thought. Or is it? How exactly do we daily make choices that are aligned with these two commandments of Christ? David and Paul would answer, "Know God. Jesus' answer summarizes 613 laws into two simple, great commandments. For those of you saying, "Hey, you said one thing. This sounds like two things!" Be patient – I am getting there.

Looking at the Ten Commandments (Exodus 20), the first four define our vertical relationship with God, while the final six our horizontal relationship with others. Looking at this a

Clicking with God

little differently we can describe the first great commandment as God's desire for a (vertical) relationship with Him and the second His desire for our (horizontal) relationship with others. Remember, within days of this proclamation Christ is crucified on the cross; the same cross that now stands at the center of history. The same cross dimension of the cross illustrates our relationship with God. The horizontal? Our relationship with others. The cross is not the cross unless you have both. This is a beautiful and simple illustration of God's will for our lives. His one thing for our lives.

    Christians seemingly enjoy making a career out of complicating God's will for their lives. It is clearly God's will for us to be saved. The problem is that many of us do not want to be saved – it feels too much like we are losing control of our own lives. Before we commit and "lose control" we want to know the day-to-day details. Should I marry this person or that person? Should I take this job or that? Should I go to Taco Bell or Wendy's? Are we there yet? God must find it humorous how we get mired down in the details instead of simply walking. We don't consider all the ergonomics, kinematics, nervous system communications and inner ear balance requirements that are all firing simultaneously when we walk. We just walk. To make it more complicated is really unnecessary. God's desire is for us to be living in both dimensions to the fullest. This is exactly what Paul is saying in his letter to the Philippians.

    All of us are on a journey. The question is to where? How often do we as Christians react to the unexpected by assuming the worst? When faced with difficult choices all too often we choose easy and fast over integrity and sacrifice. At other times though, our heart may say yes but our feet say no.

Choices, Choices, Choices: Life's Proverbial Forks In The Road

Excuses such as "I can't" or "I don't have time" or "Not now" dominate our responses. How often do we fail to turn to the One resource who has laid out our path? How often have we failed to trust Him and when relying on ourselves failed, simply given up? More times than not it is simply a case of not waiting on God. It is not the trials at the crossroads that create our problems. It is often our choices amidst the trials.

The human (self) desire is to avoid negative outcomes which all too often stir up some very odd reactions in us. My favorite example of this is when Pilate chose to free the terrorist Barabbas (Luke 23:19), and allow the innocent Jesus to be crucified (Luke 23:22) all to maintain order within a highly volatile Jerusalem. What makes this so interesting to me is the name of the terrorist. Barabbas (Bar Abbas) literally translates as "son of the father". So the guilty "son of the father" was released and the innocent "Son of the Father" was condemned and gruesomely executed. When we find ourselves at the crossroads of decision we must remember to root our choices in the love of Christ rather than our own convenience and selfishness. Sooner or later we will be left staring at a bare cross and a hard choice: His will or ours?

One final point, do you remember the encounter with the fig tree? Jesus did not just throw that in at this point in the Matthew narrative (21:18-22) without a purpose. Our true love for God must translate into love for others. One of the critical dangers to the Church today is that too many believe that being a Christian stops with only the vertical relationship. However, we must bear fruit. When Jesus was crucified His arms were stretched out in the horizontal and nailed to the cross. They extended not to receive the nails that temporarily held him to the cross, but to receive all of us in an embrace of love. If we truly love God and accept His embrace of love we become members of the 'Body of Christ'. And it is this 'Body of Christ' that continues to reach out to others both within the community of faith and to the lost.

Let's not complicate Christianity. Let's keep it simple – as God intended. Our one thing must be God's one thing: Love the Lord your God with all your heart and mind and strength; and love your neighbor as yourself. This is not two things but one. They are not sequential but circular. They are interdependent. They are one thing. I fully recognize that keeping our eye on this one thing is not always an easy thing to do, perhaps never an easy thing to do. If we claim to be Christians we must become His hands and feet to our communities. We must be beacons of Christ's light to a darkened world. We must be living examples of the Gospel of Truth.

So how is it going for you today? Are you focused on God's one thing for your life? When we make choices based on our love for God and others, our paths becomes clearer. Our choices are not only about being called to be a missionary to Africa but to be a living witness in our neighborhood. It is not only about serving on a work and witness trip to Haiti, but also helping a co-worker who lost her husband put up a basketball hoop for her ten year old son. Regardless of our choices God is with us. But for each of us this journey begins at the crossroads where one direction (choice) leads to a new relationship with God and the other remains an orbit about our self.

Chapter 8

From In Adam To In Christ Justified Through Faith

Christ is much more powerful to save, than Adam was to destroy.

John Calvin

"We are justified, not by giving anything to God, - what we do, - but by receiving from God, what Christ hath done for us."

William Gurnall

Therefore, since we have been justified through faith, we have peace with God through our Lord Jesus Christ, through whom we have gained access by faith into this grace in which we now stand. And we rejoice in the hope of the glory of God.

Romans 5:1-2

I know very few people who do not relish the smell of a good campfire. There is just something about being in the great outdoors and taking in the aroma of crackling hardwood that is almost intoxicating. When camping, I would look forward to waking early and emerging from the tent to rekindle the dormant fire and thaw the morning chill. Extinguished the night before, one could not help but to notice the different fragrance which blanketed the doused, charred wood. It was not the enticing aroma of the night before, but more the odor of ruination crying for new life. Our sense of smell triggers certain memories. Some are pleasant and others not so much. While a campfire immediately reminds me of many wonderful camping trips, the smell of doused, charred wood is a fragrance redolent of another, much more despondent event I remember far too well.

The morning's sunrise could not dispel the despair and hopelessness in the city. The battle that raged over the past several days had left a wake of burnt out buildings, schools with shot out windows, and row after row of deserted and looted businesses. Home to millions this portion of the city had been reduced to a shadow of its former self. The city-wide curfew had finally been lifted and a large, dark SUV slowly made its way up the once traffic riddled boulevard. Only the occasional curious car or armed military personnel still patrolling the area expelled the notion that this had become one enormous ghost town. While the government had stated it was safe, it was still with some sense of trepidation that the SUV ventured forward into an area of the city that would shock many. While the scene is reminiscent of the war torn Berlin, Germany in 1945 or Sarajevo, Bosnia-Herzegovina in 1995 this one hits a bit closer to home: South Central Los Angeles, 1992. It is an event that I will never forget. For those of you who may not remember this or were too separated to fully appreciate what took place let me give you a bit of historical context. While a long history of racial strife and gang warfare frequented this area of Los Angeles, this particular event was sparked by two truly regrettable events resulting in justifiably mounting perceptions of a total lack of justice which spiraled into what would become known as the LA Riots.

Rodney King had a long and storied history of criminal behavior including robbery, drugs and alcohol abuse, the rest of the world was introduced to him when he, an African-American, was severely beaten by a handful of white police officers in March of 1991, after being pursued and pulled over for speeding. The beating, lasting nearly 15 minutes, resulted in devastating injuries to Rodney King and was caught on film by a private citizen. The tape made its way to the LA media where it was replayed over and over again, making National and International news and adding credibility to the historic accusations of police brutality and racial profiling in the city.

Less than two weeks later, in a completely separate event, Latasha Harlins, a 15-year old, African-American girl was accused by a Korean store owner, Soon Ja Du, of stealing an orange juice while she was approaching the counter to pay. After a short, physical confrontation between the Du and Harlins a gun is drawn and Latasha Harlins was shot in the back of the head, killing her instantly. Two weeks, two painful events. Two cries for justice. The trial and verdict against Du was delivered that fall, to the incredulous ears of the community Du was only sentenced to five years of probation and a $500.00 fine. Only a spark was needed to light the flames in this divisive city, and that is exactly what happened.

The following spring four police officers charged in the beating of Rodney King were acquitted. The flames ignited into an explosion of anger and frustration. Within minutes riots began at the corner of Florence and Normandie and raged for six days, resulting in the death of more than 50 people and over $1 billion in damages to the community. People demand justice! When it goes the way we think it should we are happy. As an example, I believe that a vast majority of Americans believe that Osama bin Laden "got what he deserved". However, when it does not go the way we desire, such as with the Rodney King or Latasha Harlin trial verdicts, it ends with the LA Riots.

Take a look at all of the criminal investigation shows on television right now, Law & Order, CSI (and its many subsets), NCIS, Justified, American's want justice. However, if we are being honest with ourselves, our notion of fairness and justice applies to everyone . . . except ourselves. Have you ever gotten what you didn't deserve? Have you ever *not* gotten what you *did* deserve? All of us have experienced some level of perceived injustice as the officer pulls us over and presents the speeding ticket when we were *only* doing 40 in a 30. I mean, everyone does that, right? However, when we roar past the cop on the highway doing 85 in a 65 and he pulls out to nab the guy behind us, we often don't slow down. We merely keep a better look out for the next radar trap.

Growing up, my younger brother Michael, and I shared a bedroom. One day the relentless temptation overtook me to use my pocketknife and I began to carve away at the door casing of our bedroom closet. That door molding exemplified a great frontier for me that day, and I was determined to hone my pocketknife skills while leaving my mark on history. Dinner at our house always followed the same routine, my brother, sister and I would quickly respond to our mother's call telling us dinner was ready. We would all be seated at the table and then wait. Wait for my father who took our arrival as his cue to begin washing up for dinner. On his way to the washroom, my father would pass my brother's and my bedroom. Something caught his eye that night, and he promptly came to the table demanding to know who had decided to desecrate the door molding. Silence. My brother did not know what I had done, so his silence was expected. My silence, on the other hand, was purely out of fear. In a shear stroke of luck (for me) my father, tired of the deafening silence, issued judgment, picked up my younger brother, and hauled him off into the hallway, proceeding to spank him. I can still hear him crying out, "I didn't do it!" That day my brother got what he did not deserve, while I didn't get what I had truly deserved.

Fast forward some 35-years. The entire family is sitting in my parents' living room after a wonderful dinner together, reminiscing and sharing stories. I finally fessed up to my good fortune that night at the dinner table. However, my father did not remember the event at all, but my brother did! Forty years old and far removed from that night, he remembered the injustice. As I finally admitted my guilt my brother stood and only half-jokingly exclaimed to my father, "I told you I didn't do it!"

> **For the wages of sin is death, but the gift of God is eternal life in Christ Jesus our Lord. (Rom. 6:23)**

This is what we deserve. We have all sinned. We deserve the wages for our actions, and the wage for our actions is death . . . .eternal separation from God.

> **For all have sinned and fall short of the glory of God. (Rom. 3:23)**

What about Jesus? What did He deserve? Did Jesus deserve to be Crucified? Absolutely not! Jesus got what He did not deserve, in order for us to *not* get what we *do* deserve. And here is the point over which many a person stumbles: There is nothing you can do to deserve it. You can only accept this free gift of grace.

> **For it is by grace you have been saved, through faith—and this not from yourselves, it is the gift of**

> God—not by works, so that no one can boast. (Eph. 2:8-9)

If you open any number of the Bibles which I have carried and marked up over the years, you will see a big heart encircling Romans 3:21-31 and in the margin the note "The heart of the Gospel", the Good News! In the Church we call this Salvation.

> This righteousness from God comes through faith in Jesus Christ to all who believe. There is no difference, for all have sinned and fall short of the glory of God, and are justified freely by his grace through the redemption that came by Christ Jesus. (Rom. 3:22-25)

Our salvation is initiated at that point in time when we confess and believe (Rom. 10:9). It is at that moment we are justified by God, and the gift of the Holy Spirit begins to sanctify us, set us apart, which will be completed in glory, our glorification.

>Justification.
>> Sanctification.
>>> Glorification.
>>>> In that order.

Let's take a moment to reflect on just exactly what Christ did for us on the Cross.

Justification is a legal declaration of *not guilty* where the merits of Christ's sacrifice on the Cross for our sins are credited to us. Christ died for us! This substitutionary atonement satisfies God's law, the just penalty of the law, and removes our guilt. It also reestablishes our relationship with Him. The infinite chasm created by sin which separates us from our Creator, has been bridged by the loving act of obedience by Christ on the Cross.

> And by that will, we have been made holy through the sacrifice of the body of Jesus Christ once for all. (Heb. 10:10)

It is very important to always remember that the sole basis for our justification is Christ and his atoning death. Christ died for our sins to justify us before God in the final judgment. He died for us so that we could live for him. Paul discusses this in much more detail in the fifth chapter of his letter to Rome.

> Therefore, since we have been justified through faith, we have peace with God through our Lord Jesus Christ, through whom we have gained access by faith into this grace in which we now stand. And we rejoice in the hope of the glory of God. (Rom. 5:1-2)

As Paul continues this letter he deals with the Biblical doctrine of "the two Adams" (Romans 5:12-21). As I read and studied this particular section of Scripture, the immense amount of theological discussion and debate where nearly every phrase has been contested could not be missed. However, despite the questions this passage raises, Paul's primary point is quite practical. We have a universal problem, and God has the solution.

Paul ties the problem, sin, to the first Adam. He then secures the solution to the second Adam, Jesus Christ and His atoning sacrifice on the Cross.

Two men: Adam and Christ
Two actions: Disobedience and Obedience, even to the Cross
Two declarations: Judgment and Grace
Two conclusions: Separation and Justification
Two rulers: Sin & Death and Grace & Life

Christ is the basis for the solution the problems, pitfalls and predicaments discussed in the earlier chapters. He is the solution to sin, death and separation from God. Barclay's[12] title for his section commentating on Romans 5:12-21 is short, simple and correct: *Ruin and Rescue.*

I know there are many that really struggle with this Biblical truth. They say, "Not fair! Why should Adam's disobedience result in consequences for me? Why am I being held responsible for something someone else did?" This response is totally normal and totally human. In fact, this question is actually a form of one of the most common questions regarding God and the Christian faith: Why does God allow bad things to happen to good people? People far smarter than I have penned entire books on this singular question, so I will not attempt to fully unravel this deep mystery in a few paragraphs, however, let me summarize two thoughts that have always helped me.

First, God could have created His world free of sin and suffering, but in order to do that He would have had to eliminate our free will. Put another way, if we were to be truly free, God had to allow for the possibility that we would make bad choices. And we all have. While this short exposition may address the bad things humans do to one another, the second thought helps with those horrible events that appear to be totally out of our control. Things like cancer and natural disasters. God is in the business of maturing his followers. This sanctifying process is more than God's desire for morally free creatures. He also desires for us to grow and develop, and that can only be accomplished as we face difficult moral choices in a world that contains a pretty high level of evil and suffering.

> And we know that in all things God works for the good of those who love him, who have been called according to his purpose. (Rom. 8:28)

---

[12] Barclay, William: The Letter to the Romans. Louisville: Westminster John Knox Press, 1975, p77.

Think about it for a minute. In order to produce the highest level of moral development trials would be required. How could courage or sacrificial love be developed in a world devoid of evil and suffering?

A dear friend of mine has a powerful testimony that may illuminate this hard truth. As a young man he contracted the still lethal disease called Rocky Mountain Spotted Fever. His testimony detailing the lengthy ordeal he faced in the hospital and his literal flirtation with death is gripping. The physical damage done never fully healed and has affected many aspects of his life, even 30 years later. However, what made an indelible mark in my memory is how he views that trial. My friend is not bitter. I have never seen him down about what could have been. Instead, his living testimony regarding a gracious God has always left the question in my mind: Could I do the same? My friend even goes so far as to say he would not go back and change a thing, for you see during his extended hospitalization a relationship developed with the staff and at least one nurse came to know Jesus Christ as her personal savior as a result of my friend's witness. God used my friend's trial for His glory. That is what Paul is talking about in Romans 8:28. Those trials are also the fire God used to further refine my friend, strengthening and maturing his relationship with his Heavenly Father. Was that fair of God? Maybe not from our vantage point, but is God faithful? Absolutely!

> For since by a man came death, by a man also came the resurrection of the dead. For as in Adam all die, so also in Christ all shall be made alive. (1 Cor. 15:21-22)

Adam's sin is the unwanted gift, but the grace of Christ is our undeserved gift if we accept it.

So how is your fire burning? Have you accepted God's free gift of grace to kindle the flame of the Holy Spirit within you? Or are you content to remain but a doused shadow of your true spiritual potential, never to realize or experience the power of a relationship that clicks with your creator. Previously I shared this illustration of how I viewed my relationship with God several years ago at that youth retreat where I was speaking. What I have learned over the past months (actually nearly two years) as I have studied and authored the book you are now reading is that this image needs to be tweaked.

For the justified believer I believe that Christ begins the sanctifying process the moment we accept His gift of grace. However, I still have my toys, my old habits and sins, which I attempt to hide from Him and occasionally take out to play with. This new image is a better visualization of that level of relationship. Unfortunately this is the image that represents a vast majority of Christians today.

As Christians, God is calling us to so much more. For me He was calling me through those "feelings". I began feeling that there was something more to my faith, my relationship with Him that I was not experiencing. He is calling each of us to take the next step with Him where we leave the toys behind, climb onto His lap and allow Him to guide and direct our lives. The Father creates the plan for our lives, Jesus Christ initiated the plan at the Cross, and the Holy Spirit will faithfully administer the plan.

Over the next three chapters let's walk with Christ, learn to run with the Holy Spirit and eventually dance with our Heavenly Father.

> Father Instituted
> > Christ Implemented
> > > Spirit Empowered

The Good News is that if you are a Christian you are already somewhere on this journey. It is a journey which does not afford us the option to be couch potatoes. God is calling us out of our comfort zones. It is our daily choice whether or not we continually heed His call.

Chapter 9

Walking With Christ
One Small Step For Man,
One Giant Leap For Mankind

'If you are seeking creative ideas, go out walking. Angels whisper to a man when he goes for a walk."

Raymond Inmon

"Me thinks that the moment my legs begin to move, my thoughts begin to flow."

Henry David Thoreau

I am the vine; you are the branches. If a man remains in me and I in him, he will bear much fruit; apart from me you can do nothing.

John 15:5

It was a beautiful morning on the eastern shore of Florida as Apollo 11 lifted off from Launch Pad 39A at the Kennedy Space Center at 9:32 AM EST. Attached atop a Saturn V rocket with over 5,000,000 pounds of total propellant on board, Commander Neil Armstrong, Command Module Pilot Michael Collins, and Lunar Module Pilot Edwin "Buzz" Aldrin, Jr. were launched on one of the grandest journeys in the history of mankind. Four days later the lunar module would descend and land on the Moon in the Sea of Tranquility. Several hours later, on July 21st at 10:56 pm EST Neil Armstrong put his left foot on the rocky Moon and stated, "This is one small step for man, one giant leap for mankind." I was four years old so I do not remember Neil Armstrong's famous first step on moon in 1969.

It had been just over eight years since President John F. Kennedy announced before a special joint session of Congress, the ambitious goal of sending an American safely to the Moon and back before the close of the decade. The U.S. had met the ambitious goal of a President who tragically did not live to see it accomplished. President Kennedy firmly understood the magnitude of the challenge he had issued in 1961. At an address at Rice University in 1962 he famously stated, "We choose to go to the moon. We choose to go to the moon in this decade and do the other things, not because they are easy, but because they are hard . . . because that challenge is one that we are willing to accept, one we are unwilling to postpone, and one which we intend to win, and the others, too."

For years many skeptics have gone on record that we never went to the moon. They claim that the photos, audio and video coverage were all staged. There is even an episode of Discovery Channel's Mythbusters which busts the myth saying that the famous image of Neil Armstrong's lunar footprint is a forgery, given that scientifically it is not possible in a moistureless vacuum to leave a footprint that detailed. For many, certain things are hard just to accept or to believe. Two thousand years ago another historic journey took place. This journey has had more skeptics than any other. It was a journey from death to life. The resurrection of Jesus Christ is a journey from death to life, from the cross to the grave, from the grave to the sky. He is risen!

We are called to join Christ on this journey to life. This is the trajectory of grace we talked about in the last chapter. Whether you call Him Savior or simply view Him as one more mythical character, He still desires to walk alongside you; every day and every moment. Your decision to walk or not walk with Christ does *not* change His decision to walk with you. Luke tells the story (Luke 24) of one such occasion, on the day of Christ's resurrection. After appearing to Mary Magdalene, Jesus chooses to appear to two of his disciples as they made the short seven mile walk from Jerusalem back home to Emmaus. These two followers of Jesus had been with the larger group of disciples when Mary Magdalene burst in to the upper room announcing that the tomb was empty and angels had told her that Jesus was alive. They stayed behind while Peter and John ran to the empty tomb. But after Peter and John returned, confirming Mary's story, and before Christ appeared to the group, they had left. Why? Did they believe the news was too good to be true? Did they think it was all a hoax? I believe the answer is found in verse 21.

> "We had hoped that he was the one who was going to redeem Israel." (Luke 24:21)

Disappointed. Dissatisfied. Disillusioned. It had been a good ride, but even as the initial trumpets of triumph announced His resurrection, they packed up and went home, deciding it was time for a fresh start; a new journey. They had followed Jesus thinking he would redeem Israel. They thought he would overthrow the Romans and reestablish the House of David. They believed Jesus was dead, and that all of the stories and wild claims were just that, stories.

Why would Jesus appear to these two before appearing to the remaining eleven apostles (remember Judas Iscariot had already committed suicide)? Doesn't this sound a lot like the Parable of the Lost Sheep? Leave the 99 to find the one, or in this case leave the nearly 500 to reveal yourself to the two. And that is exactly what Jesus did. While the two journey home, discussing the events of the past three days, Jesus takes the initiative to walk alongside them. They do not recognize Him, as He walks and talks with them, patiently teaching them, reminding them, explaining why the Messiah had to suffer and die. As they arrive in Emmaus Jesus begins to continue past the town, testing the two for a response. They invite him in to eat (sounds a bit like Revelations 3:20 to me!). It is not until they are sharing dinner that Jesus opens their eyes, and reveals Himself as the risen Christ. He then promptly vanishes. Their disillusion, disappointment and dissatisfaction are instantly gone, and the two followers, reinvigorated by the encounter, immediately get up and head back to Jerusalem where they share their wonderful experience with the other disciples.

It sounds incredible, unbelievable, and too good to be true. It must be a hoax. Dead people just don't wake up after three days and magically walk around the countryside, randomly appearing and disappearing. Do they? As Christians we not only believe in the Resurrection, we are called to follow our risen Savior and join Him on His journey (not ours). Still today, two thousand years later, we who call ourselves Christians are to watch for what Jesus is doing around us and join Him! Impossible? No. Difficult? At times. Alone? Never. Our new journey, His new trajectory of grace for our life, does not promise continual comfort. However, Christ does promise to walk with us. Just like the two dejected disciples walking the road to Emmaus, Jesus comes alongside to walk the byways of our day to day life with us. This is actually the road to "perfection" (spiritual maturity). It is the pursuit of holiness. It is the daily quest to become more like Jesus. And all of this is possible as we walk with Him.

Jesus talks beautifully about this side by side relationship in the fifteenth chapter of the Gospel of John. The following verse summarizes how Jesus defines this new relationship with Him, using the imagery of the vine and the branches.

> I am the vine; you are the branches. If a man remains in me and I in him, he will bear much fruit; apart from me you can do nothing. (John 15:5)

He is the true vine; we (believers) are the branches. Jesus is the source of life and strength, we are to bear fruit. What does it mean to bear fruit? I used to always associate bearing fruit with evangelism, and that is part of it, but it is more. The fruit is the Fruit of the Spirit.

> But the fruit of the Spirit is love, joy, peace, patience, kindness, goodness, faithfulness, gentleness and self-control. Against such things there is no law. (Gal. 5:22-23)

As branches, we are the visible Body of Christ – the Church with a capital C! We are His hands and His feet.

Love for the lost
Joy for the disappointed
Peace for the restless
Patience for the frustrated
Kindness for the cruel
Goodness for the wicked

Faithfulness for the disbelieving
Gentleness for the grieving
And self-control for the selfish

What Jesus begins, His Church continues. Just imagine if the Fruit of the Spirit were consistently evidenced in your church, in your life. It sounds almost utopian. Is this even possible? Yes, but only through Christ, the Vine. Only as we continue keep in step with Him.

> Since we live by the Spirit, let us keep in step with the Spirit. (Gal. 5:25)

Since our relationship is defined by the vine, our response must be to stay connected to that vine.

The gospel of John communicates this truth and is the very heart of Jesus' illustration.

> Remain in me, and I will remain in you. No branch can bear fruit by itself; it must remain in the vine. Neither can you bear fruit unless you remain in me. (John 15:4)

This is our Christian responsibility. The King James Version (KJV) uses the word "abide" in place of the NIV's choice of "remain." I have always preferred abide. Remain sounds static, while abide has the sense of belonging – like I am home. Whether translated to abide or remain, what is clear is John's fondness for this term. He uses it over fifty times in his writings, eleven of which are in this chapter alone. Abiding is important to John – as it should be to us! This concept of walking with Jesus, joining Him on our new trajectory of grace, is really about abiding. Staying connected to the vine is not a static but rather a dynamic relationship. Faith leads to a healthy dependence upon Christ, the source of our strength. It is a dependency resulting in spiritual fruit! Abiding - his voice, our choice - is essential for fruit bearing.

As you continue through the John chapter 15 there is a second dimension of our 'abiding' where Jesus says,

> "As the Father has loved me, so have I loved you. Now remain in my love." (John 15:9)

Abiding in Christ (vv. 4-8) stresses faith and dependency. The emphasis in these verses is on obedience; an obedience to abide in his His love. The obvious question at this point is how. How do we remain in His love? Jesus continues in the next verse with the answer.

> "If you obey my commands, you will remain in my love, just as I have obeyed my Father's commands and remain in his love." (John 15:10)

Obedience. The best example of this kind of abiding is found in the life of Christ, as His life was one of complete obedience to the Father. The author of Hebrews writes,

> Let us fix our eyes on Jesus, the author and perfecter of our faith, who for the joy set before him endured the cross, scorning its shame, and sat down at the right hand of the throne of God. (Heb. 12:2)

If you only remember one thing from this chapter, let it be this. Obedience is *not* just about following rules, or doing what we are told. This is an obedience that results in our joy (v. 11). Walking with Jesus, abiding in Him and His love, is about experiencing God's love in and through Christ.

As Jesus is saying these things to His disciples, he is mere hours from His crucifixion. God's ultimate demonstration of love will imminently be witnessed by the disciples, as His Son is crucified, laying down His life for His friends. If the love of Christ is to be shown in His disciples, they must be willing to give themselves to and for others. Jesus says,

> "My command is this: Love each other as I have loved you. Greater love has no one than this, that he lay down his life for his friends." (John 15:12-13)

Abiding in Christ allows us to experience God's love and to express that love to others. Why do we struggle to simply abide? A primary reason is our preoccupation with independence. We want to experience His power, but fail to experience His person. I remember someone once stating that we desire guidance but ignore the Guide. We seek answers to prayers instead of recognizing Him as *the* Answer.

The famous poem, 'Footprints', has long been very dear to me. I view my inconsistent Christian walk during college as a time when there was all too often only one set of footprints. It was a time of significant spiritual struggles for me. It was a time when I believe that Christ not only walked alongside me, He carried me. I have had a framed version of the poem hanging in my office for years, as a reminder of God's faithfulness to me. Recently there has been a lot of buzz about this poem as some clever folks added a new ending to the poem which I really like, but I will leave that for the next chapter.

Chapter 10

Dancing With God
Discovering His Rhythm

I would believe only in a God that knows how to dance."
Friedrich Nietzsche

David, wearing a linen ephod, danced before the LORD with all his might, while he and the entire house of Israel brought up the ark of the LORD with shouts and the sound of trumpets.
2 Samuel 6:14-15

Therefore do not be foolish, but understand what the Lord's will is.
Ephesians 5:17

Frederick Nietzsche is best known as one of the world's most colorful advocates of atheism. His quotes and writings litter the pages of books written over the last century. Intelligent and audacious, Frederick Nietzsche had been the youngest chair (at the age of 24) of historical literary and linguistics studies at the University of Basel in Switzerland. This brilliant philosopher believed God never existed for a number of flawed reasons, and that Christianity was "the greatest of all conceivable corruptions . . . the one immoral blemish of mankind."[13] I have often wondered how the trajectory of Frederick Nietzsche's life might have been altered had his father, a Lutheran pastor, not died when he was only four years old. One wonders if scars resulting from the death of his father had some impact on his beliefs and that if his father had lived, he would not have spent his life proclaiming that God is dead, he would have believed that God does dance.

I believe God dances. I don't mean the waltz, mambo, samba or cha-cha-cha. And let's be clear, God does not prance, shimmy or strut. But boy does God move. God is always moving. Moving around us. Moving in and through us. Always leading and asking us to follow. Have you ever truly *felt* His presence? Have you *heard* Him speak? Have you *seen* Him move? I mentioned in the last chapter the creative ending to the classic poem Footprints that I like so much. As the trail of footprints in the sands continues onward they

---

[13] Friedrich Nietzsche, *Anti-Christ,* trans. H. L. Mencken (New York: Knopf 1920), p. 230.

become disorganized, chaotic. They are not even footprints anymore, but more like gashes and worse. The individual questions the disturbing image, and Jesus calmly replies, *"That is when we danced."* I relate all too well with the single set of footprints illustrating those times when Christ has carried me. I am learning the joy of what it means to, at times, dance *with* God. Have you ever danced with God?

It was Mother's Day 1991. I had flown from California to Illinois to spend an extended weekend with my family. On Saturday we celebrated my brother's graduation from college, and Sunday I danced with God. Sunday morning found me in church with my mom, the church I grew up in. It was a packed house as a number of visitors were attending to honor the mothers in their lives. I was struck by some of the faces in the crowd that day. Sitting beside a woman I knew, was her husband who had never accompanied her to church before. Filling an entire row was my aunt and a number of my cousins, with their families. Again, I can't remember having ever seen them in church. As I scanned the sanctuary I noted other unknown faces that I was sure told similar stories. I don't remember how the service started, but I remember God clearly speaking to me that He had something special planned. It was during the first or maybe second song that I felt the overwhelming conviction to break all protocol, ignore our "liturgy" and go to the front of the sanctuary, kneel at the altar and pray. I did.

The music continued as my mom's pastor, Pastor Cable, came alongside of me and asked how he could help me pray. I told him that I believe God had something special planned for today's service, and that I was praying for His will to be done. During our time together, others started moving to the altar. Long story short the entire service was one extended time of prayer at the altar. The pastor never made the altar call, God was doing that Himself. I was overwhelmed. I returned to my seat as the people continued to come and go to the altar. I purposefully "targeted" my friend's husband and began praying for him. Within what seemed to be mere moments he stepped out, went to the altar and accepted Christ. Words cannot convey the spiritual ecstasy I was experiencing in that moment as I danced with God. I began praying for my cousin and her husband. They stepped out and went to the altar. Unbelievable! I could not contain myself. I was standing, rocking back and forth, crying out with joy. I don't remember how the service ended, but I will never forget how it started – with God speaking to me and my obedience at the altar with Him. Have you ever danced with God?

My dad has often joked about the time, years ago, when he took Arthur Murray dance lessons. Beginners learn about the three important elements of dancing; (1) foot position (2) rhythm and timing (3) leading or following. I think God would agree. The last chapter was all about the position of our feet as we walk with Christ and abide in Him.

In Chapter 4 we introduced that the beautiful word in original Greek, *Paraclete*, that John uses on several occasions in his Gospel. (14:16-17, 26; 15:26; 16:7-11; 16:13-15) It is translated in various versions of the Bible as 'Counselor', 'Comforter' or 'Advocate'. It is in these verses in John's Gospel where Jesus promises His disciples that when he departs he will send them another paraclete, the Holy Spirit. The Paraclete who will come along side us, walk with us, journey with us, laugh and cry with us. He will always be with us.

But dancing is about more than just our feet. There is a rhythm to God leading and Christians following, our hearts dancing in step with God's love. This is "clicking" with God. Have you ever danced with God? Enoch danced.

> And after he became the father of Methuselah, Enoch walked with God 300 years and had other sons and daughters. Altogether, Enoch lived 365 years. Enoch walked with God; then he was no more, because God took him away. (Gen. 5:22-24)

In these three verses twice you see the phrase, "Enoch walked with God." Enoch kept it simple. The writer is telling us something by repeating this statement. The second mention (v. 24) acts much like our modern underlining or italics to add further emphasis to the point. Say something three times and it is the equivalent of using an exclamation point! But that only happens twice in the Bible (Isa. 6:3 and Rev. 4:8); both times to describe God's holiness as *Holy, Holy, Holy!* Now it doesn't literally say Enoch danced with God, but let's be honest, a lot Christians have "walked" with God, but how many have been taken directly to Heaven before we die (Gen. 5:24)? Enoch had such an incredible relationship with God that he never died. Enoch danced all the way to Heaven with God.

What does dancing with God look like? Walking with Jesus, abiding in Him, lays the foundation for dancing. It is much like after we learn the basic footwork we must learn the rhythm and timing. It all starts with the relationship. It is absolutely impossible to dance with God without truly knowing God. Some of you reading this book know many things about God but have never started a relationship with God. Knowing about God and never starting a relationship with Him is like knowing about oxygen, but refusing to breathe. Paul and David knew this. Remember their "one thing"? To know God! We must make that "12 Inch Journey" where what we know is evidenced in how we live. God deeply desires to have with each of us the same relationship He enjoyed with Enoch. I would hope that all Christians yearn for these moments in their walk with Him, where they dance.

Far too many of us are not willing invest the time necessary for God to nurture the intimacy required to truly dance with Him. We would rather read a novel than His Word; take a nap instead of sitting in silent conversation with our Heavenly Father; wander the web instead of worshipping in wonder. Dancing with God happens as we practice His presence. How can we hear His gentle whisper, the call to follow His lead, unless we intentionally listen? As I consider the various times in my walk when I have danced with God I find myself agreeing with C. S. Lewis who wrote that:

> "It is in the process of being worshipped that God communicates His presence to men."[14]

I danced with God that Mother's Day in 1991. I have also danced with God while experiencing a sunrise at Yosemite and late one night as I drove across Michigan with my wife and son sleeping in the back seat. In each case I was worshipping God whether it was in a church, silently meditating on Him or praising Him in a song.

Have you experienced the awesome presence of God as you worship? In that moment, you felt Him closer than ever before. If you struggle to experience dancing with God, it may be because you struggle to worship Him. Never forget that it was Jesus' worship that Satan desired.

> Again, the devil took him to a very high mountain and showed him all the kingdoms of the world and their splendor. "All this I will give you," he said, "if you will bow down and worship me." (Matt. 4:8-9)

You worship the one you serve. And too often we serve our Self. I will admit that my times dancing with God are too few and far between. But to be clear this is not because God is not present. He is. He is still calling, still leading. I am simply not listening, not obeying, not following. It is *not* His presence that diminishes, but rather our awareness of His presence. Remember the vine and the branches. God is that near.

So, if God is always present is it possible to constantly dance with God? I think we all know, in our human condition, the honest answer is unfortunately no. Why not? Simply put we have too many distractions, and too little faith. We need to stop talking and start trusting. We need to stop working for God and begin working with God. So how do I sense God's leading? How can I become more familiar with his gentle voice calling out to me? The psalmist says it well,

---

[14] The Problem of Praise in the Psalms (found in *Reflections on the Psalms* [New York: Harcourt, Brace and World, 1958], pp. 90-98

> Be still, and know that I am God. (Ps. 46:9-10)

This Psalm has always been one of my favorites, and Martin Luther's basis for the Reformation hymn "A Mighty Fortress Is Our God." Take a moment, open your Bible and read it... It is only eleven verses... You have the time... Have you read it yet? It is a celebration and a proclamation. It is a resounding affirmation of our firm foundation, our security found in God's boundless strength. God is present. He desires to dance with us, but we too often fail to be still and worship Him. This psalm is a reminder that our environment and our lives are constantly in motion (remember you are moving over 1.3 million miles per hour!), and while tomorrow's circumstances are uncertain we know that Jesus is walking with us; God is present with us. Slow down and absorb what the psalmist is writing. Stop for a moment and ponder this psalm. The first nine verses are our meditation. Verse 10 is God's response which is followed by a single concluding verse. Note the progression. We meditate (worship); God responds. We stop and are still; God reveals Himself. It is in these quiet moments that we experience God; it is then that we dance with God.

The same peace of God that calmed the storm on the Sea of Galilee can calm our hearts. We are invited to "know" God. Remember the "12 Inch Journey". "Knowing" God is to experience Him. As we still our hearts and minds we allow the peace of God to settle upon us. We will dance with Him. Let me end with a wonderful exchange I read several years ago, which perfectly summarizes what it means to dance with God. Dan Rather once asked Mother Teresa. "What do you say to God when you pray?"

Mother Teresa answered quietly, "I listen."

Taken aback, Rather tried again, "Well, then, what does God say?"

Mother Teresa smiled, "He listens."[15]

---

[15] Timothy Jones, *The Art of Prayer*. New York: Ballantine Books, 1997, 133.

Chapter 11

Running The Race With The Holy Spirit Powered Endurance

"I often wonder if religion is the enemy of God. It's almost like religion is what happens when the Spirit has left the building."

Bono

"The doctrine of the Spirit is buried dynamite."

A.W. Tozer

But you will receive power when the Holy Spirit comes on you; and you will be my witnesses in Jerusalem, and in all Judea and Samaria, and to the ends of the earth.

Acts 1:8

The American proverb states, "Success is a ladder you cannot climb with your hands in your pockets." It is ingrained in the American belief that every individual has the opportunity to move up the social ladder and prosper. One of the greatest examples of this is Thomas Edison. In Edison we find a true rags-to-riches story of a poor, self-taught boy who grew up to be the greatest inventor of his time, arguably, of *any* time. Seventy years after his death, he still holds the record for the greater number of US Patents ever awarded to an individual – 1,093. Known to sleep an average of four hours a night, surviving only on short cat-naps throughout the day, Edison periodically worked for seventy-two hour stretches in order to perfect an invention.

One of Edison's most famous quotes is "genius is one percent inspiration and ninety-nine percent perspiration" where he captures both his work ethic and drive precisely. Over the years many other individuals have left unattributed quotes on this popular topic. Some of my personal favorites include:

> "All the so-called 'secrets of success' will not work unless you do."
> "Some people dream of success. . . while others wake up and work hard at it."
> "The difference between try and triumph is a little 'umph'."
> "Those at the top of the mountain didn't fall there."
> "The view is better when it is earned."

But my favorite may be the Chinese saying:

> "Man stands for long with mouth open before roast duck flies in."

While I have no issues with the relevance of these sayings, in many aspects of our lives, if applied to our salvation or relationship with God they create a fallacious optimism of heavenly expectations. Far too many Christians sadly live their lives believing basketball legend Larry Bird's statement, "I've got a theory that if you give 100 percent all of the time, somehow things will work out in the end." Trying harder alone does not guarantee success. "If only I had tried harder, done more", we hear this all the time. If only I tried harder I could lose weight, get a promotion or better grades. If only I had done more my marriage wouldn't be in shambles. If only I had paid more attention a loved one's suicide or addiction could have been avoided.

In regards to our relationship with God, simply trying harder is at its best misguided and a consistent source of frustration in the life of the Christian. If we view our Christian journey as an attempt to climb the ladder of success we eventually discover that the pursuit is both relative and fleeting. So often we compare our faith with that of those around us as if it is some sort of competition. Living the victorious Christian life is not some sort of Olympic competition. Have you ever tried to see how far you could jump? For most of us it would be somewhere around 6-10 feet. So if we could jump 11 feet we would feel pretty good about ourselves. That is until one learns that US Olympian Mike Powell holds the world record at almost 30 feet. All of a sudden my 11 foot long jump pales in comparison. Our relationship with God is not based on the relative merit of our own abilities. God is calling us to be Christ-like. That is like asking us to jump the Grand Canyon. It is beyond human capability - at that point, whether you can jump 10, 11 or even 30 feet, it is totally irrelevant.

Do you remember the story about Sisyphus from Greek mythology? He was the mythical king of Corinth who was eternally punished in Hades by having to roll a large rock up a hill, but each time as he neared the top the rock would roll back to the bottom. Like Sisyphus, when we set out to establish our relationship with God, by merely trying harder, we never reach the goal.

> Not by might nor by power, but by my Spirit,'
> says the LORD Almighty. (Zech. 4:6b)

This verse is God's message to Zechariah to be given to Zerubbabel, the governor of those who have returned to Jerusalem from the Babylonian exile. It is a stark reminder to them, and to us, whatever we attempt will only be accomplished by the power of the Holy Spirit. Zechariah and his fellow travelers would remember the complete fiasco that resulted when earlier Israelites returning from exile attempted to construct the temple (Ezra 3:8-13).

If victorious Christian living is not the result of trying harder to climb some ladder of righteousness, how can we experience it? Well, the irony of ladder climbing is that the further you climb and the harder you try, the further you get from the answer. Salvation is not "up there" but right here at the bottom of the ladder! Salvation, in the form of Jesus Christ, came down the ladder to us, to walk with us and us with him. And as we continue to walk with Him we begin to learn how to dance with God. But again, the question is how? If the American proverb, "Success is a ladder you cannot climb with your hands in your pockets", is truly misplaced in regards to our relationship with God what simple truth captures the reality of how?

Instead of ladder climbing – doing, obeying, striving – the author of Hebrews compares the Christian journey to a race.

> Therefore, since we are surrounded by such a
> great cloud of witnesses, let us throw off everything

> that hinders and the sin that so easily entangles, and let us run with perseverance the race marked out for us. (Heb. 12:1)

It is a race that is more a marathon than a sprint. In chapter 9 we shared how our ability to walk with Christ (Gal. 5:25) is predicated on our responsibility to obediently abide in Him (John 15:4). And in the previous chapter we discussed the secret to joyfully abiding is found in our willingness to fall in rhythm with our Heavenly Father. And as we said this is only possible as we become aware of and follow the Holy Spirit, the Paraclete, the Spirit of Christ who comes along side us, walks with us, journeys with us, laughs and cries with us. He is always with those who believe. Jesus did not ascend to Heaven to watch from afar, but left his very Spirit, the Holy Spirit here with us. The very last words of Christ recorded in Scripture convey this truth.

> But you will receive power when the Holy Spirit comes on you; and you will be my witnesses in Jerusalem, and in all Judea and Samaria, and to the ends of the earth. (Acts 1:8)

God's plan of salvation, His plan for all of our lives, is:

Father Instituted
    Christ Implemented
        Spirit Empowered

Yet, how often do we bypass this third truth – that it is God's plan for each of us to be Spirit empowered. Far too many believers fail to realize the Spirit empowered Christian life because they fail to relate to this third person of the Trinity. For many of us we can relate to a Heavenly Father and His Son Jesus Christ, but the Holy Spirit by His very name is a bit too abstract. We end up settling for two out of three. Yet it is the Holy Spirit who has been sent to be our primary helper!

The majority of Christians today, who are not simply ignoring the Holy Spirit, treat Him as some sort of supernatural power to tap into. While it is absolutely true that the Holy Spirit is here to empower us, it is to empower us to carry out God's will, not our own. It is only possible to walk with Christ when we strive to remain in step with the Spirit (Gal. 5:25). How much easier it is to be in step with Him if we have a relationship with all of Him! But how exactly does one do that? How do we stay in step with something we cannot see and can barely describe? The answer lies in the fact that we only see (or hear) what (or whom) we are expecting to see or hear.

A previous employer of mine had every staff member participate in a multi-day workshop to discover the key to unlocking human potential in order to significantly improve both personal and organizational performance. There were many exercises from that training course that I have continued to use to this day, when I teach. One particular exercise was based on a discussion about a mental capability we all have, something called our Reticular Activating System (RAS). Now, I could repeat what they taught me in the class about our RAS. I could tell you it is functions from the brain stem and that it plays a role in awareness and perception. I could also tell you that the RAS is basically a switch that can be made aware of certain stimuli and cause our cortex to respond. Instead let me give you a couple of examples where each of us has already experienced our own RAS at work.

You know the drill. You buy a new bright blue Ford Fusion and then wham, you begin seeing them on the road everywhere. Why is that? Your RAS! Before buying the car you were not "looking" for other blue Ford Fusions, but simply making the conscious decision to purchase that make, model and color causes your RAS to subconsciously tell your cortex to begin acknowledging all of the other similar cards that had previously been hidden in plain sight. How about going through a noisy supermarket or airport terminal? You may or may not be aware of the constant background noise around you and the endless unrecognizable chatter coming over the intercom.

That is until you clearly hear your name called. How can your brain ignore or not perceive all the other words that were spoken, but clearly pick up the instant your name is called and immediately grab your full attention? Correct, your RAS! Your RAS takes your conscious instructions and passes them on to your subconscious. In our airport example the instruction was to listen for your name being announced. It is no different with the Holy Spirit. If we are to recognize the activity of the Holy Spirit in, around and, hopefully, through our lives we need to be better at perceiving Him. That is exactly how God created us to function.

Our inability to see or hear the Holy Spirit in our day to day lives is not the result of His lack of effort, but rather our lack of perception. So how do we change that? Before I answer that question I feel obligated to make it clear that this is not some simple, hocus pocus, positive thinking short cut. Every Christian has been promised the Holy Spirit, and as Christians we can begin to better perceive Him all around us as we daily exercise our spiritual muscles. We call these exercises spiritual disciplines. There are many types of disciplines and include time in prayer, Bible study and the memorization of Scripture. They are the exercises to consciously communicate God's truth and enable our ability to perceive Him. Just as physical exercise develops and hones our muscles, spiritual disciplines develop our inner being; the being which transformed the moment we were saved. Paul states this truth well in his second letter to the church at Corinth.

> Therefore, if anyone is in Christ, he is a new creation; the old has gone, the new has come! (2 Cor. 5:17)

These disciplines equip our new creation to better perceive the Spirit by faith, not merely by sight (2 Cor. 5:7). As redeemed believers they not only afford us the ability to perceive the Holy Spirit working within and around us, they equip us to obediently evidence His character and His thoughts in our outward behavior.

Sounds simple doesn't it. But before we trivialize this solution let me remind you that exercising these spiritual disciplines is a daily decision to listen to His voice not our own, and this daily process is a spiritual battle. This is the last thing Satan wants you doing. Paul describes this raging battle in all Christians very well in Romans 7-8. In these two epoch chapters Paul simply looks around him and sees both his and our daily Christian struggle with sin. While separation from God was completely addressed for all time at the Cross, we can still feel the pull of sin and disobedience to God. So many Christians find themselves in Romans chapter 7 wanting to live righteously but actually choosing the exact opposite. These two chapters are laying bare before us the two natures at war within us. As new creations in Christ our challenge is to progressively reject that old relationship to self and sin. A simple word search of these two chapters provides the foundation for our answer as to how this can be accomplished. Take a moment and read these two chapters in Romans and note how many times you see the word "I" in Chapter 7 and the word "Spirit" in Chapter 8.

In Romans 7 (NIV), a chapter detailing Christian struggle and repeated failure, the first person pronoun, I, is used a whopping 33 times while the Spirit is never mentioned. Not once! Moving forward to Romans 8 we see the victorious, sanctified Christian life. Here I is used only twice while the Spirit is mentioned 17 times. I trust you see the obvious truth, if we continue to try to live our lives based on our own abilities and efforts we fail. However, if we yield to the Spirit we can increasingly live the victorious life to which we are called. We can only move from the Chapter 7 self-righteous and striving ladder climbing struggle to Chapter 8's victory if we diligently incorporate the spiritual disciplines in our daily lives. It is this faithful approach to our daily Christian lives that enables us to both perceive and be empowered by the Spirit so that we can walk with Christ and dance with God. It is not enough to just go to Church to hear a 30 minute sermon, we must daily put His Word into action in our lives (James 1:22), and His power is available to do just that. In fact, it is often literally right beneath our feet!

There is a well-worn preacher's illustration that I have heard on more than one occasion that illustrates this truth. Located in West Texas is the small town of Iraan which owes its odd name to a Great Depression sheep rancher Ira Yates and his wife Ann. The Great Depression had so totally sapped Mr. Yates fiscal resources that he was no longer able to pay any of his bills. Things had become so desperate that he was on the verge of losing his ranch and sheep, his only remaining source of income. It was then that a truly serendipitous series of events changed everything. An oil company's seismograph crew ventured into the area and explained to Mr. Yates that there may be oil on his property. After signing a simple contract an exploratory wildcat well was drilled and at just past 1000 feet, "up from the ground came a bubblin' crude. Oil that is, black gold, Texas tea."[16] Well, unlike TV's *Beverly Hillbillies* this is a true story, and the first well pumped out over 75,000 barrels a day. Years later the wells were still pumping out over 100,000 barrels a day. And Mr. Yates owned it all. In today's terms at $100 per barrel that equates to $10,000,000 per day of oil! The truth is that the day Mr. Yates put pen to paper and purchased that land he owned the rights to all of that oil laying right beneath his feet. He was standing on a fortune yet living on government assistance and on the verge of losing everything. He was literally a millionaire many times over living in abstract poverty. He owned the oil, but could neither perceive its existence nor conceive how to access it.

In regards to the Holy Spirit the same can be said for many Christians today. While we know and believe that Christ died for us we struggle to experience the daily joy of truly living for Him. The simple truth is that Christ died for us so that we can live for Him. The last two chapters shared our need to

---

[16] http://www.lyricsondemand.com/tvthemes/beverlyhillbillieslyrics.html

both abide in Christ and truly worship our Heavenly Father. This is only possible when we are empowered by the Spirit.

> Empowered by the Spirit
>> Abiding in Christ
>>> Worshipping the Father

Please note that we are called to abide and we respond in worship, but it is the Holy Spirit who empowers! So often we get this backwards. Instead of being empowered by Him, we struggle on our own. In one of my absolute favorite books regarding the Holy Spirit, Dr. Charles Stanley shares his insights regarding this struggle when he reminds us that we are called to be bearers, not producers, of the fruit of the Spirit.[17] When we are called to abide in Christ it is His Spirit that abides in us. It is the Holy Spirit that empowers us to joyfully live Christ-like lives.

However, He is not announcing Himself with wild shouts but in whispers (1 Kings 19:12) and waits for us to perceive *and* respond. We will only experience the true joy of our faith when the Holy Spirit moves from being incidental to fundamental in how and who empowers our journey. Jesus left us with His power to live, but it is a power we cannot wield. It is a power that can only be transmitted through our lives *after* we yield to His Spirit. The Holy Spirit is available for you. For the remainder of this book I want to walk through some means to both practice His presence and apply these principals to a life that clicks with God.

---

[17] Stanley, Charles: *The Wonderful Spirit Filled Life*. Dallas, Tex.: Thomas Nelson, 1992, p65.

Part III

Practicing His Presence

Living a Life that is Clicking with God

Chapter 12

Living In The Third Dimension Gaining His Perspective!

There is safety in complacency, but God is calling us out of our comfort zone into a life of complete surrender to the cross. To live dangerously is not to live recklessly but righteously. And it is because of God's radical grace for us that we can risk living a life of radical obedience for Him.

Steve Camp

For the eyes of the LORD range throughout the earth to strengthen those whose hearts are fully committed to him.

2 Chronicles 16:9

I have been crucified with Christ and I no longer live, but Christ lives in me. The life I live in the body, I live by faith in the Son of God, who loved me and gave himself for me.

Galatians 2:2

Have you ever flown a plane? I tried once, only once. While I obviously lived to tell the tale, it was neither graceful nor enjoyable. Roy, my college roommate had taken flying lessons and received his VFR (Visual Flight Rules) license which allowed him to rent and fly a plane - weather conditions permitting. As with most college students, money was not an abundant resource, and my roommate needed to accumulate flight hours which required renting a plane. He was always looking for someone to go up with him (and split the bill). On a couple of occasions I took Roy up on his "offer" and took to the skies above central Illinois. What a perspective to understand how truly flat this area of God's creation is.

On one such occasion I had the idea to fly approximately 75 miles northeast to Kankakee where my sister was going to college. The plan included picking up my sister and her friend, and then bringing them down to Champaign for the weekend. We would then fly them back to Kankakee on Sunday. Did I mention we were only 22 years old? Oh to be young. Actually, my parents would have flipped if they knew some of the stuff we did in college! (Sorry Mom and Dad) While bad weather forced me to drive and pick them up, we were able to fly them back on Sunday. And that is where this story really begins. After safely returning my sister and her friend to the campus airport, Roy and I climbed back in the small Cessna (or Piper or whatever it was) and took off to fly home.

Once airborne Roy asked if I wanted to try and fly the plane. Absolutely! Let me pause here to state that there is a *big* difference between driving a car and flying a plane. Unless something terrible happens, cars are meant to operate in two dimensions. I can go forwards and backwards, left and right. Planes, on the other hand, are designed to operate in three dimensions. You also can go up (ascend) and down (descend). Going up is fairly straight-forward. Going down? Well that can be a bit more stressful, especially when trying to land. Flying a plane requires coordination and control of your pitch (the nose of the plane going up or down), the roll (the wings "rolling" up and down) and the yaw (the plane "turning" left and right). In short, this is very difficult for a novice. After a few seconds (seemingly minutes) of failed attempts to keep the plane level and on course Roy thankfully took back the controls and returned us safely home. While I was excited to take hold of the controls I was more than relieved to relinquish them.

All of the details required to pilot the plane were ruining my ability to enjoy the ride. Moving from driving in two dimensions to flying in three dimensions is very difficult without a lot of qualified instruction. It is not until we tap into this qualified instruction that we can enjoy the view without being distracted by the details. The final chapters of this book will move from talking about how to click with God to actually living a life that clicks with God. We view our day to day lives in two dimensions: time and location. We have busy lives. We have dentist appointments, tee times and business meetings. We have to meet our child's teacher at school tomorrow afternoon at 3, and we have to make it home for dinner at 6. You get the idea.

To live a life that clicks with God, we need to add the third dimension of *what*. What would God have me do in that time and location? Yes, we are going to the teacher conference to hear about Johnny's progress in 2nd grade, but how does God view that encounter? What would transform that encounter into a time where we click with God? This can be difficult to grasp, but God desires to elevate our Christian lives, to give us a new perspective – His perspective. God is continually reaching out to us and calling us to a higher ground, a life in this third dimension, an opportunity to see His plan for our lives, His creation. Jesus gives us a wonderful example of this truth. If you are Jesus and you want your disciples to experience this same elevated perspective, how do you do it? You can't quite take them up in a plane, but you can take them up the mountain. Remember my adventures in inversion rappelling? Even upside down I was able to take in the view. And if you are going to take your disciples up the mountain you may as well pick one of the biggest, right? And so Jesus did!

Standing at over 9,200 feet above sea level is the historic Mount Hermon. It is located about 40 miles north of the Sea of Galilee and marked the northernmost boundary of Israel at the time of Christ. No matter where you are in Israel if you look north your view is terminated by the snowcapped peak of Mount Hermon. Today, called *Jabal el-Shaykh*, it stands along the current border between Syria and Lebanon. Parts of her southern slopes still extend into the northernmost boundaries of the hotly contested Israeli occupied region known as the Golan Heights. On these slopes is the historic city of Banias, also known as Panias.

Panias, and the surrounding region, historically steeped in the worship of Baal, was later conquered by the Greek Seleucids about 200 years before Christ. With them they brought their stories and worship of Pan, the pagan god of nature. Hewn directly into the faces of surrounding cliffs, visitors to the area can still view the remains of a temple built to Pan. Panias would later come under Roman rule, and Roman Emperor Caesar Augustus would later grant this region and the city to Herod the Great, who subsequently built a temple there to Caesar Augustus. Following Herod's death, his son Philip assumed control of this region and renamed the town to Caesarea Philippi, in honor of (Caesar) Tiberius and himself. It is to this city, on the slopes of Mount Hermon that Jesus brought His disciples (Matthew 16) for a lesson in perspective and to witness of living in the third dimension.

Visualize the setting. Jesus and his disciples arrive at this border town where the people of Israel met the people of the Gentile world. The disciples would be well aware of the Old Testament history of the region. The Canaanites, who inhabited this land prior to the return of Israel from Egypt, worshipped numerous false-gods including Baal. Now, overlooking the city, Jesus and the disciples see beautiful gardens and tree lined paths which crisscross the town connecting the impressive temple to Caesar and the various sites of Pan Worship. This is the setting Jesus chose to reveal His higher perspective, a life in the third dimension, an opportunity to see His plan for their lives, and ours. And it started with a simple question captured by all three of the synoptic Gospels.

> When Jesus came to the region of Caesarea Philippi, he asked his disciples, "Who do people say the Son of Man is?" They replied, "Some say John the Baptist; others say Elijah; and still others, Jeremiah or one of the prophets. But what about you?" he asked. "Who do you say I am?" Simon Peter answered, "You are the Christ, the Son of the living God." Jesus replied, "Blessed are you, Simon son of Jonah, for this was not revealed to you by man, but by my Father in heaven. And I tell you that you are Peter, and on this rock I will build my church, and the gates of Hades will not overcome it." (Matt. 16:13-18

It only took Jesus one question to reveal His higher perspective, His plan for their lives . . .and ours! Jesus tells His disciples to look around. They see temples to Caesar and Pan. They see a region historically lost to pagan worship. Can they see beyond these false gods? Peter can. He boldly states the truth that Jesus is the Christ, "the Son of the living God" (v. 16). Jesus then builds on this confession with the introduction of something new, the church (*ekklēsia*). It is the first use of this word in the New Testament. It can be translated as "those called out" as representatives. Christ's official representatives. The Church is *not* a building, but rather a committed community of believers in Christ. We, the redeemed, are the Church. The Church is the primary means by which God will make Himself known to the world.

One of the most overlooked phrases in this scripture is the last nine words of verse 18. We all seem to notice Jesus' proclamation to Peter that he is the rock at the beginning of the verse but miss Jesus' proclamation to us at the end when he says, "And the gates of Hades will not overcome it." Are gates for offense or defense? Defense of course. Jesus is saying that Hades is on the defensive and it will fail. The Church is to be on the offensive. Christ was establishing His Church and the Caesars, Pans and other powerless gods of Hades would not prevail against it. Praise God! But Jesus was not done.

In the very next chapter in Matthew He reveals the life in the third dimension in a most dramatic way. It is the life required of the Church.

> After six days Jesus took with him Peter, James and John the brother of James, and led them up a high mountain by themselves. There he was transfigured before them. His face shone like the sun, and his clothes became as white as the light. (Matt. 17:12)

Undoubtedly, one of the purposes of the transfiguration was to afford the disciples the opportunity to see Jesus in His true glory. But I also believe that it was so these disciples could realize a whole new dimension of Christ – His eternalness. There is far more to Christ than simply His human body. Christ is God. He is immortal. He is pure.

In between these two events: the confession of Christ and the Transfiguration, are three verses forming the very essence of God's plan for our lives, the Church and His creation. It is this call to third dimensional living that is the great lesson. Not just in eternity, but today and tomorrow.

> Then Jesus said to his disciples, "If anyone would come after me, he must deny himself and take up his cross and follow me. For whoever wants to save his life will lose it, but whoever loses his life for me will find it. What good will it be for a man if he gains the whole world, yet forfeits his soul? Or what can a man give in exchange for his soul? (Matt. 17:24-26)

Dying, losing one's life, does not come naturally. As we discussed earlier in the book too many see these verses as too burdensome. They see a call that is totally unrealistic. All of us have an innate will to live. And beyond just existing we all desire to leverage our time and talents to live life as fully as possible. We desire to fulfill our dreams, to love and be loved and to leave a legacy for our children. For these reasons, these verses are some of the hardest in the entire Bible. There must be some easier explanation than what appears to be painfully obvious. One of the challenges when you read Scripture is that what we are reading is a translation of the original. In the Greek there are three different words that all appear as the word "life" in our Bibles: *bios*, *psyche* and *zoe*.

Now, *bios* is the Greek root for the English word biology - the study of "life" and is most aligned with our understanding of life today. When I was asked my freshman year in high school to answer the question, "What is life?" on my science class final exam it was concerning *bios*. However, in scripture it is the least used. In the entire New Testament it is only used ten times and often to simply denote our physical bodies. Time is the enemy of *bios*. Getting older does not make our bodies better. They are in a continual state of decay. We can exercise and eat right - which we should - but in the end our *bios* will expire. We cannot live without *bios*, but the New Testament warns us that we ought not to live for it. God is not concerned with *what* we have but rather *who* we are. And this leads to the second Greek word for life – *psyche*.

Psyche is the root of our word psychology. It is not the study of the body, but rather the study of the mind, and behavior. *Psyche* refers to that life which does concern God - *who* we are. While *bios* describes life *psyche* characterizes it. It is our true nature. While time is the enemy of *bios*, the enemies of *psyche* are apathy, complacency, and the tyranny of the urgent. It is our *psyche* that God desires to transform – to transfigure. What Jesus is saying in these verses is that we must part with one thing in order to gain another. "For whoever wants to save his *psyche* will lose it, but whoever loses his *psyche* for me will find it." (v. 25). If we are to live in the third dimension we must be willing to leave the second dimension behind. But what is this third dimension?

The Greek word is *Zoe*. In John's Gospel Jesus says, "Whoever loves his life [psyche] loses it, and whoever hates his life in this world will preserve it to eternal life [zoe]" (John 12:25). If we make life, what (bios) and who (psyche) we are, *zoe* eludes us. Only in the surrender of our *psyche* to Jesus Christ can we preserve *zoe*. Only in giving up what we have and what we are, for what we might become, do we receive by God's grace, *zoe, eternal life*. *Zoe* is the life that characterizes God, and also the life that God wills us to share with his people. *Zoe* is the third dimensional living God is calling us to. It is the life that Jesus was describing at Caesarea Philippi. It is God's one thing for us.

So, if time is the enemy of *bios* and apathy the enemy of *psyche*, what is the enemy of *zoe*? Sin. The Bible is clear on this from the very beginning. The Septuagint is the Greek translation of the Old Testament. In the Septuagint Genesis tells us of the "tree of life (*zoe*)" (Gen 2:9) located at the center of the Garden. God's plan has always been that we would live in this third dimension. That we would live in communion with Him, that we would experience *zoe*. The sin that separated us from experiencing this life has been bridged by the death and resurrection of Jesus Christ. We are called to receive this life from God. It is a free gift by faith. This gift of *zoe* changes our perspective. We begin to see that our lives- both what we have (*bios*) and who we are (*psyche*) – are called to love and serve God. To love and serve others. To resonate.

Paul resonates with Christ when he writes these majestic verses in his letter to the church at Ephesus.

> I keep asking that the God of our Lord Jesus Christ, the glorious Father, may give you the Spirit of wisdom and revelation, so that you may know him better. I pray also that the eyes of your heart may be enlightened in order that you may know the hope to which he has called you, the riches of his glorious inheritance in the saints, and his incomparably great power for us who believe. That power is like the working of his mighty strength, which he exerted in Christ when he raised him from the dead and seated him at his right hand in the heavenly realm. (Eph. 1:17-20)

Much like Jesus at Caesarea Philippi, Paul desires to bring us to a higher place, a place of Godly perspective. He desires for us to see the panorama of hope in which we are called. God has a grand, expansive plan to bring all the disorder of sin under the order and rule of Christ. It is the plan to restore wholeness: Wholeness of communities, wholeness of families, wholeness of nature itself, wholeness of all things, wholeness of you, and wholeness of me. His plan, the Church, is fulfilled as believers demonstrate the power of the Cross, the power of forgiveness, the power of love to others. This power is available to all of us, here, now, today!

To click with God, to resonate, to participate in the restoration of wholeness we must practice His presence. The poet Elizabeth Barrett Browning beautifully captures this concept in her classic poem "Aurora Leigh".

> Earth's crammed with heaven,
> And every common bush afire with God;

> But only he who sees, takes off his shoes,
> The rest sit round it and pluck blackberries.[18]

I don't know what you see in the bushes around you — the consuming fire of heaven or mere blackberries. It is truly a question of eternal perspective. We must continually practice His presence, and in doing so discover that His perspective is taking hold of our lives. Then, and only then, will we begin to see others as Christ sees them. Let's now look more deeply at how we "Practice His Presence". Now that we have talked about the "what's" (what is clicking with God, what does it mean to resonate, and what does it mean to live in the third dimension) let's explore some "how's". How do I resonate in my worship? How do I click in my community? Each chapter is a dance lesson. The dance begins when we look inward and engage with God in the process of becoming more and more Christ-like.

---

[18] Elizabeth Barrett Browning, "Aurora Leigh," no. 86, lines 61-64, quoted in Nicholson & Lee, eds., *The Oxford Book of English Mystical Verse* (London: Oxford, 1917).

Chapter 13

Living Dangerously Facing The Right Way!

"If you could only sense how important you are to the lives of those you meet; how important you can be to the people you may never even dream of. There is something of yourself that you leave at every meeting with another person."
Fred Rogers

"Until he extends his circle of compassion to include all living things, man will not himself find peace."
Albert Schweitzer

But he wanted to justify himself, so he asked Jesus, "And who is my neighbor?"
Luke 10:29

If you have ever visited the Alsace region of France you have had the privilege to take in the beauty and wonder of this historically contested slice of land along the Rhine River which defines France's current border with Germany. My former employer had their European operations located just outside Strasbourg in the tiny town of Duppigheim – or was it Duttlenheim. Many find it odd to see the concentration of German sounding towns in this region of France, but one only has to remember that Alsace has gone back and forth between the Germans and the French on four occasions over the past 200 years. It should be no surprise that Alsace is also home to most of the infamous Maginot line. My visits are too numerous to count, but they always left me ready for the next. My preference was to stay in one of the quaint hotels in nearby Ottrott or Obernai. It was like visiting a postcard. I always enjoyed seeing the Strasbourg Cathedral (Cathédrale Notre-Dame-de-Strasbourg), the occasional day trip to the nearby Haut-Koenigsbourg Castle, or a long lunch in one of the historic walled villages located along the Route du Vin (wine trail).

However, one of my most relaxing times each day was the morning and evening drives to and from our offices. While you could zip up the A35 freeway towards Strasbourg and quickly arrive at our facilities I typically choose the more casual drive through the Alsatian countryside. My chosen path was typically D35 toward Griesheim where I would then zig and zag from one country road to another. The path took me through a handful of small villages with wonderful squares and half-timbered houses. Adding to the ambience were numerous, simple roundabouts with vintage signs pointing in various directions stating the next village down each road. I can hear some of you saying, "Roundabouts? I hate those things!" I think you would like these as other cars were few and far between, and the roundabouts were simple two lane opportunities to simply hit the clutch and accelerate to the next tree lined road. With that said, I will completely agree that other roundabouts or traffic circles can be maddening if not life threatening; one only has to look a four or five hour car ride away to Paris.

Paris is the number one tourist destination in the world. Combining a population of over 10 million with a large percentage of the 80 million annual tourists descending on France, to say Paris is a bustling city would be an understatement. People, scooters, cars, taxis and buses are everywhere! One quickly learns to ditch the rental car option and ride the Paris Metro and the occasional taxi cab. However, even in a taxi my blood pressure would go off the charts when we had to navigate the Place Charles de Gaulle. If you don't know the name you would recognize it in a photograph. It is the roundabout servicing the intersection of twelve avenues, including the famous Champs-Élysées, encircling the Arch of Triumph. With around 10 lanes of traffic and twelve connecting streets where more cars are attempting to come and go it is not uncommon to take multiple loops attempting to get to your appropriate exit. You can literally become trapped driving in circles. Circles. Thanks Euclid!

Circles are everywhere. Like Stonehenge and crop circles they can be mysterious, like a wedding ring they can be beautiful, and like roundabouts they can create tranquility or turbulence. Let me tell you about one more circle. About fifteen years ago my church was going through a difficult and extended pastoral transition. Long story short, it took nearly nine months to find our next shepherd. During the interim we had a retired pastor fill the pulpit most Sundays. My most prominent memory from his time at our church took place during a Sunday evening service. The church had reached about 800 in attendance under a previous pastor, but conflict and divisiveness within the church had sent that number tumbling until we were closer to half that size. On Sunday nights we were lucky to have 100 attending. As the service drew to a close Pastor Irwin had the congregation stand and form a circle. In a sanctuary built to hold over 1,000 it was not difficult to do. As we formed our crude "circle" Pastor Irwin stepped down from the platform and walked to the middle of the sanctuary. Once he arrived at the middle of our circle he stopped and we all watched him waiting for some closing word of insight. After a short pause, he began to trace the circle making eye contact with each and every one of us. He then announced, "You are facing the wrong way!" You see, we were doing what all of us would do when asked to form a circle – we faced inwards toward each other.

Too often the church forms an inward facing circle. Too often we become more of a country club than an emergency ward. We build new sanctuaries and gyms. We develop the next great program. Unfortunately these wonderful creations far too often suit our tastes much better than they do the Great Commission (Matt. 28:18-20). Facing inward also places our eyes firmly on each other instead of on the lost. One of my favorite songs is a classic by Steve Camp called *Living Dangerously in the Hands of God*. During the song Steve Camp speaks the following statements:

> There's safety in complacency, but God is calling us out of our comfort zone into a life of complete surrender to the cross. To live dangerously is not to live recklessly but righteously. And it is because of God's radical grace for us that we can risk living a life of radical obedience for Him.[19]

---

[19] Steve Camp, *Living Dangerously in the Hands of God*

There is safety in our little circles at church. In our circles we can choose who is in and who is out. We make the rules. We get comfortable.

But God is calling us out of our comfort zones. He is calling us to face the right way. He is calling us to stop asking for only what we want and to begin accepting what we truly need; to stop making up the rules and begin obeying His commands. He expects us to be His Church! God is calling us to His Mountain to gain His perspective, to grasp His vision for creation, and to move into His fields. The Great Commission says "Go" not "Come". It is an outward facing, ever expanding, actively penetrating mission. Jesus is saying today what He told his disciples,

> "The harvest is plentiful but the workers are few. Ask the Lord of the harvest, therefore, to send out workers into his harvest field." (Matt. 9:37-38)

This little passage forms a bridge between the ministry of Jesus (Matt. 5-9) and the ministry for His disciples (Matt. 10).

As a result of Jesus' teaching (Matt 5-7) and numerous miraculous healings (Matt 8-9) a large crowd had gathered around Him. He is touched by their suffering and expresses compassion for them. Whether for the masses or the disciples, Jesus' ministry is always based on compassion. Christ's compassion goes well beyond sympathy, even beyond empathy. His compassion always results in caring action.

> When he saw the crowds, he had compassion on them, because they were harassed and helpless, like sheep without a shepherd. (Matt. 9:36-37)

Like sheep without a shepherd. Jesus deliberately paints a picture of hopelessness, confusion, and despair. Leveraging Micaiah's prophetic and grave announcement to Ahab (1 Ki. 22:17) He is bringing focus to the spiritual lostness of the crowds. Like sheep without a shepherd, harassed by the wolves and unable to help themselves, they have no shepherd to guide and protect them. Not only were the religious leaders, who should have been their shepherds, maligning these sheep they were keeping them from following the true Shepherd.

Note Jesus' first call to His disciples – pray (Matt. 9:38). Never lose sight of the fact that it is God who is the Lord of the harvest – not us! God is the vine, we are the branches. We are God's husbandry (1 Cor. 3:9) not the other way around. It is God who chooses where, when and for how long the called will work. We are called to pray that those God calls follow. And when we pray, be prepared to be called! Our prayers should be made with the same spirit as Isaiah when he said, "Here am I, send me." (Isa. 6:8). Only after praying for God to send us should we ask for God to send others. Instead of determining our own commission, commissions given in answer to prayer are more likely to be successful.

This commission, the Great Commission (Matt. 28:18-20), is more than just preaching or being a missionary to Africa. It is about evangelism and disciple-making and discipleship. Don't fall prey to analysis paralysis and make this command overly complicated. It is about simple obedience. I have often used the St. Francis of Assisi quote, "Preach the Gospel at all times and when necessary use words." He believed he preached while he silently walked through a market being observed by those he passed. He would say, "It is of no use to walk anywhere to preach unless we preach everywhere we walk." The Great Commission is God's call to make a spiritual difference in the lives of others.

We live in a world that quite literally depends on people helping people. We can easily recall illustrations of this in the near past: hurricane Katrina hitting New Orleans in 2005, the devastating earthquake in Haiti in 2010 and the tsunami-earthquake-Fukushima nuclear disaster trilogy in Japan in 2011. In each case you literally saw people from all over the world come together to supply food and aid. You see it in Kuwait and Kosovo when nations unfairly attack another. We truly need each other. Without compassionate people, civilization would simply spiral into chaos. We have been created, called and commissioned to *go* and make a difference in the lives of those around us. When we are simply obedient to this call and commission, we too experience a deep joy and a wonderful difference in our own lives. Grasping this truth addresses the effects of the Pareto principle which is alive and well in our churches today. Better known as the 80-20 Rule, the Pareto principle states that 80% of the effects result from 20% of the causes. In business this means 80% of sales come from 20% of customers. In your church it means that 80% of the financial giving and volunteering of time and talent comes from 20% of her members. Sadly, this means that 20% of Christians experience the joy of this simple obedience to God's call to go. Stated simply 80% of us are facing the wrong way. Are you facing the right way?

Everyone needs someone to reach out to them with a hand full of the love of Christ. There is no better way to strengthen your heart than to lift someone else up in the love of God. Jesus didn't say go and be happy. He didn't say go and make money. He didn't even say go to church and then go home. He said go and make disciples. The word disciple means one who embraces and assists in the spreading of a teaching. Disciples face the right way! Look through the Bible. The people who made a difference were not necessarily people of great talent or knowledge. They were just average people like you and me who were honest and sincere. Moses and Jonah actually resisted trying to help others because they were reluctant to get up and go, or get up and do. For those of you who think you are not qualified look no further than two Biblical teenagers: David who went from shepherd boy to king, and Mary the mother of Jesus. God does not call the qualified, but he does qualify the called.

Moses, David, Jonah, Mary. Look at the differences all these people made. None were qualified. But they did have one thing in common. What was it? They all had a heart that loved God and a desire to serve Him. It doesn't matter how

Living Dangerously Facing The Right Way!

big a laundry list of excuses you come up with, if you do His work, you will reap a reward better than our minds are able to understand. Too often, we aren't willing to work for God because we are very comfortable people, and in our comfort, we expect God to come down and let us work for Him in the way we find, well – the way we find most comfortable to us. This is not how God works. God expects each one of us to sacrifice. He wants us to step out of our comfort zones so that we will have to depend on Him. God uses people like us. Has God used you to touch others? Would you want God to use you as His special envoy to help others? If you want Him to, He will, but you have to be willing to let God use you. Are you living dangerously? Oh, how we should be living dangerously in the hands of God.

I previously mentioned a time I danced with God during a sunrise devotional in Yosemite. I had recently volunteered to help with the church youth group and the summer of 1994 offered me the opportunity to join their annual trek to Yosemite National Park. Each day began with private devotional times and ended with a time of fellowship around a campfire. In between we were able to explore the rugged beauty of this American treasure's spectacular granite cliffs, waterfalls and streams. I found myself daily watching rock climbers scaling El Capitan or simply taking in the majesty of Half Dome. However, it is my Friday devotional and final campfire time with the youth group that will forever be etched in my mind as a time when I danced with God and experienced the overwhelming difference simple obedience to His call brings.

Surrounded by the splendor of Yosemite I enjoyed my early morning hikes searching for quiet places for my devotionals. What I had not enjoyed was my inability to hear God's response to a very specific request. I had been offered a job in Michigan with Ford Motor Company; an offer I selfishly wanted to accept. My newlywed wife's family was in Hawaii, and mine was near Chicago. We each had two weeks of vacation which almost all went to visiting family. Admittedly, visiting the in-laws in Hawaii is nothing to complain about, but it left little time for us to do much on our own. In addition, Ford's offer was 20% higher than my current salary meaning we would be able to afford a home in Michigan much sooner than in Los Angeles. However, in addition to volunteering in this youth group I had just been elected to the church board, and I was actively working with Laotian youth at our church plant in Long Beach. How could it possibly be God's will for me to leave this harvest field? The spiritual tension I was feeling was real and went well beyond my thoughts of career and family. All week this topic had dominated my morning devotional time without an answer. Bible in hand I walked into a grassy field that Friday morning not sure if an answer would ever come.

I reclined back in the knee high grass and gazed up at the still shadowed granite faces that surround the park awaiting the morning sun. My devotional routine that week included reading some random scripture while I witnessed the rising sun slowly illuminate the western cliff face. In seeming frustration I remember letting my Bible fall open, hoping some magical verse would be exposed to me, one that would answer all of my questions and quandaries. It was as I opened my Bible that Friday morning that I simply and almost audibly heard God say, "Put the book down." As I laid my still open Bible face down on my chest I could feel my heart racing. I tried to relax and I found my gaze affixed to the distant cliffs. As the sun rose the line between light and shadow would slowly descend down the cliffs. The view was spectacular, but hearing God share, "This is my good-bye gift from California to you. Go!" was overwhelming. I will not lie; I am getting quite emotional even as I type this story now 20-years later; the morning that I once again danced with God.

That night around the campfire only the youth pastor and his wife knew of my decision to move to Michigan. As I sat quietly and listened to several of the teens share about their morning devotions I found myself moving from one teen to the next with simple prayers for each. One of the teens was an 8th grade boy named Johnny. Johnny was one of the first youths

I mentored. His parents were divorced, and I enjoyed my role as "big brother" taking Johnny and a couple other boys out for pizza, to a movie or simply hanging out with them. As I prayed for Johnny the circle grew quiet, and I decided to share my experience from that morning. After I had finished Pastor Jim took the opportunity to pray for me, my new job and the transition. He asked if there were any other prayer requests. Johnny raised his hand. This tough little boy, through tears and sobs, offered his prayer request, "That Jon would stay." I had no idea of the impact my obedience to God had had on him. In that moment I felt the overwhelming joy of simple obedience.

Chapter 14

Living In His Fields
"Earning The Right"

―☙―

"There are many of us that are willing to do great things for the Lord, but few of us are willing to do little things."
John Wesley

Sow your seed in the morning, and at evening let not your hands be idle, for you do not know which will succeed, whether this or that, or whether both will do equally well.
Ecclesiastes 11:6

The alarm rang and he begrudgingly dragged himself out of bed and headed towards the bathroom to get ready for another day. Another day, another donut . . .maybe two. However, years of too many business dinners, too much fast food, and too little exercise had taken their toll. The man in the mirror was screaming for help, and for the first time, in a long time, our bleary-eyed friend agreed. The following day he trekked to the local fitness center with a renewed desire for exercise and weight loss. He had explored this path before, but never exhibited the necessary perseverance to succeed. As he entered the fertile fields of the nautilus machine, dumb bells, and treadmills it was clear he was in over his head. Where to start? He had no idea. However, age had granted him enough wisdom to know that without guidance he would only embarrass, and quite possibly hurt himself. He needed help.

Fortunately for him, unfortunately for his wallet, this gym offered assistance in the form of personal physical trainers. These young men and women were poster children for fitness, and they were available to guide you through the maze of machinery and help you with a program suited just for you. Did he have a choice? He approached the desk where he was introduced to a recently hired trainer. What a coincidence. It was almost as if they were meant to meet. The trainer was a physical specimen: Confident, borderline arrogant, but quiet – almost removed. Over the next 45 minutes measurements were taken, questions were asked and a shallow dialog began. One of the questions the trainer asked our friend was how he had heard about this particular fitness center. He hesitated. The answer was simply that it was across the street from his church, and he had always debated joining. But does he get "religious" and say that?

He decides to jump in and responds honestly, "I go to church across the street." To his amazement the trainer says that he has noticed the church sign.

Should our friend probe? He boldly proceeds and asks, "Do you go to church?"

A nerve is obviously struck as the trainer's face visibly withdraws. His response hints a mild disgust and bluntly states, "No, I am not interested in any 'God stuff'" making it clear this line of conversation is closed.

The remainder of the session proceeds in relative silence and concludes with our odd couple doing some final stretching before they head their separate ways. Our friend is convicted to say something, anything, but what? What if he gets mad? What if he asks a question our friend can't answer? Maybe silence is the best strategy. However, deep in his heart he knows that is not what God is asking him to do in that moment.

After what seems like an eternity, our friend finally says, "If you ever want to talk about this 'God stuff" I would be happy to listen." The first seeds were thrown.

Step back 2000 years. A large group of people walk along the shore of a large lake, following a man who has been making headlines in the area with miraculous healings and a radical message about the nature of God. Explaining how we have all missed the important signs that God gave us through the centuries, that he cares about what's in our hearts, not what we do. The man gracefully steps into a boat and moves out into the shallow waters so that the crowds can better hear him teach. He is already viewed as a significant teacher, and today he is sharing a number of short stories, parables, to clearly communicate some basic truths.

Living In His Fields "Earning The Right"

Again Jesus began to teach by the lake. The crowd that gathered around him was so large that he got into a boat and sat in it out on the lake, while all the people were along the shore at the water's edge. He taught them many things by parables, and in his teaching said:

> "Listen! A farmer went out to sow his seed. As he was scattering the seed, some fell along the path, and the birds came and ate it up. Some fell on rocky places, where it did not have much soil. It sprang up quickly, because the soil was shallow. But when the sun came up, the plants were scorched, and they withered because they had no root. Other seed fell among thorns, which grew up and choked the plants, so that they did not bear grain. Still other seed fell on good soil. It came up, grew and produced a crop, multiplying thirty, sixty, or even a hundred times." Then Jesus said, "He who has ears to hear, let him hear." (Mark 4:1-9)

For Jesus, the parable is a comparison drawn between something common, found in everyday life and a spiritual truth. These parables are not intended for deep rational analysis, but rather for an intuitive, "gut" response. In fact the Greek root of the word, "parable" is the same from which we get the mathematical term, "parabola." A parabola (sorry for another nightmare geometry flashback) is a curve that gets closer and closer to a limit line, without ever actually touching it. The analogy is apt. Each of Jesus' parables gets very close to a single spiritual truth, but they never actually tell you what to do. Jesus always leaves us the responsibility to draw the final conclusion and to take personal responsibility for the actions that inevitably must follow if we take His teaching seriously. I taught teenagers for almost fifteen years (and adults for the last 10) and in both cases one of the best teaching tools is the word picture. Simply put, parables are powerful word pictures.

Over the years I have heard the debate concerning who is the target audience of this particular parable. Is it the sower, the one sharing the Gospel, or the four soils, those hearing the Gospel? The correct answer is both. To communicate the responsibility of the believer this is the Parable of the Sower. To prepare them for the various responses they will come across this is the Parable of the Four Soils. This shows the flexibility of the parable, which demands that the listener engage his or her own mind to draw the obvious analogy, and the genius of Jesus, the master storyteller. Jesus is teaching about the highly coupled topics of sowing (evangelism) and germination (making a decision to enter into a relationship with God). The quality of the soils cannot be isolated from the one sowing the seed nor those who reap the harvest. In this parable Jesus captures the entirety of this truth. Note that the sower is freely sowing seeds regardless of where they land. It is a point we should not dismiss lightly. The Great Commission (Matthew 28) specifically commands us to go to "the entire world and preach the gospel". It is not our job to pick and choose, but to simply go.

I grew up in a home, the oldest son of two parents who were children of the depression. A key phrase around our home was "waste not – want not". So, this idea of "wasting" seed that doesn't hit fertile soil appears to be a waste of our time and energies. The flaw in this line of thinking is that it is not our job to determine which soil we believe to be fertile versus thorny. How those seeds take root and grow will be determined by the choices of those listening and the ongoing work of the Holy Spirit. Each person will respond differently. It is this range of responses that often scare off many Christians from sharing. However, we need to learn to be patient with those who are not yet ready to respond. If we are not, we are in danger of preselecting those whom we believe are ready and we will miss the true opportunity. Gauging a person's readiness to be responsive is more than skin deep and it is truly a job that only the Holy Spirit of God is equipped to do.

Anyone who has heard me teach will recognize my phrase "Earn the Right" (some of my friends prefer the phrase "Experience the Privilege"). By this I mean that we must each earn the right to discuss an issue as personal as one's relationship to one's creator with another person. Evangelism should be personal and best occurs one-on-one in an environment of trust. We need to put in the time to develop the required foundations of trust for these ongoing conversations. It is this foundation laying effort that I refer to as "Earning the Right". We are "Earning the Right" to be trusted. We are "Earning the Right" to be viewed as authentic and loving – Christ-like. While I do agree that this process is a wonderful experience and a true privilege in which to take part, I still prefer "Earn the Right".

Now "Earn" does *not* imply that sharing the gospel is a right to be earned. Nor am I saying that we "earn" our salvation – or theirs! Paul states it very clearly in Ephesians when he writes,

> "For it is by grace you have been saved, through faith—and this not from yourselves, it is the gift of God - not by works, so that no one can boast." (Eph. 2:8-9)

It is our job to throw the seed. It is the Holy Spirit's job to convince the person of their need for God, and it is each individual's responsibility to make their own decision. The growth of God's Kingdom is the result of individual responses. Spiritual growth cannot occur unless people hear the Word, but spiritual growth will not be initiated until an individual accepts the Truth. The final step is really the process of not only accepting the Truth, but in living the Truth and bearing fruit. Paul captures this reality in his very next verse in Ephesians,

> "For we are God's workmanship, created in Christ Jesus to do good works, which God prepared in advance for us to do." (Eph. 2:10)

If we fail to recognize this progression as a requirement of walking with God we fall into what Dietrich Bonhoeffer calls cheap grace.

Cheap grace is a watered down grace that no longer even remotely resembles the grace of the New Testament. In Bonhoeffer's words

> "[It] is the preaching of forgiveness without requiring repentance, baptism without church discipline, Communion without confession, absolution without personal confession. Cheap grace is grace without discipleship, grace without the cross, grace without Jesus Christ, living and incarnate."[20]

Cheap grace is an intellectual agreement with the Truth without a real transformation in the sinner's life. It is the justification of the sinner without the works Paul says should accompany new birth. We need to "work" to develop an environment where our family, friends, neighbors, co-workers, and those that enter our circle of influence begin to be willing to dare to share, dare to question, dare to seek. However, this work does not guarantee success.

And what is success? For most of us success is measured by reaching the goal, and reaching it first. Too often the goal is measured in quantity instead of quality. Our churches count people in pews instead of transformed lives. We launch fancy new ministries with bigger budgets instead of having new neighbors over for dinner. We hire pastors based on how they "grew" previous churches instead of calling God centered shepherds. And we want this success *now*! We try to accelerate this Kingdom growth, and we are far too impatient. When God does not seem to be moving fast enough we push Him aside and take control of the wheel. Remember my brief piloting experience? While the process between seed throwing and conversion can be very fast it is most often measured in

---

[20] Dietrich Bonhoeffer, *The Cost of Discipleship,* trans. R.H. Fuller, rev. ed. (New York: Macmillan, 1960), 30.

weeks, months and often times years. We desperately need to get realigned with our Savior, to joyfully walk with Him, to resonate with Him and see the lost through His eyes. We need to rediscover that our Christian mission resonates with God and resonates with others. It is to preach the Gospel in love. Everything else is God's job.

Over the past 20-years I have attended only three churches. One was in southern California, the other two in the suburbs of Detroit where I now live. Over that time I have had the privilege to teach classes filled with people who were 13-years old on up to, well let's just say, those much wiser than myself. Teaching is analogous to sowing, and over the years I have discovered that the best teaching is almost never lecturing. Teaching is not about showing off what you know, but sharing how to live in Christ. Teaching is not an opportunity to show off our vocabulary and knowledge of theology; rather it is an opportunity to foster an environment where people, regardless of maturity, feel accepted and experience how to better walk with Christ and each other.

As I have mentioned my son, Patrick, is eight years old. It has been fascinating to watch his various wide eyed moments as he has learned to button his shirt, tie his shoes, ride a bike without training wheels, read his first words, and . . .operate a remote control (mercy!). These wide eyed moments are typically preceded with "Watch Dad!" and almost always followed by the exclamation, "I did it!" These are all wonderful events for any parent and their child. The problem is that prior to almost all of these milestones I would start by "explaining" how to do this or that in language my son could not understand. Compounding the problem I would often fail to demonstrate the required patience when he did not immediately comprehend and succeed at the task at hand.

Similarly, as outward facing disciples we need to pace and synchronize our conversations with family, friends and neighbors to God's rhythm who intimately knows and loves them all. Remember, sowing is a long stroll, not a 40 yard dash. As you walk with Christ and others, you begin to see more clearly the hearts of those with whom you engage. When they are ready to grow we need to be ready and available to continue sowing. At some point you too will witness those wide eyed moments, however, sometimes that pleasure may go to another worker in God's fields. These are those precious moments when the light bulb goes on; that "Ah Ha!" moment when they begin to understand. They are always worth the wait, even if you are not the one who gets to see it.

Here are six simple guidelines to help you improve your sowing: Be responsible, receptive, ready, real, relational and resourceful. First, be responsible. We need to take our call and giftedness seriously. Second, be receptive to God's guidance and direction, to questions and to suggestions. Third, we must be ready. Take the time to prepare ourselves. Fourth, we must be real. Every sower needs to be open, honest and vulnerable. Fifth, we must be relational. This is at the heart of "earning the right". Finally, we must be resourceful, using all the tools God has given us. In the end remember that the main thing is to keep God's one thing the main thing.

Epilogue:

It's Our Turn Now

The great task of the church is not only to get sinners into heaven, but to get saints out of bed.

Anonymous

So this is what the Sovereign Lord says: "See, I lay a stone in Zion, a tested stone, a precious cornerstone for a sure foundation; the one who trusts will never be dismayed."

Isaiah 28:16

As you come to him, the living Stone—rejected by men but chosen by God and precious to him—you also, like living stones, are being built into a spiritual house to be a holy priesthood, offering spiritual sacrifices acceptable to God through Jesus Christ.

1 Peter 2:4-6

The Incas, over their 300 year existence, were the largest civilization in North America prior to Columbus and the Spanish conquest of much of Mexico and South America. Rivaling the size of many Eurasian empires they spanned much of South America west of the Andes. While it is clear that their demise was the direct result of the Spanish conquest it is equally clear that their foundation was firmly built on a civilization that came before. Much smaller than the Inca and located primarily in Bolivia the Tiwanaku Empire was nonetheless a very advanced culture that laid much of the foundation on which the Incan Empire would eventually be built. Their capital city, also called Tiwanaku, appears to have been a cultural and religious center.

At the heart of the city is the Pumapunku temple complex which is theorized to have functioned as the spiritual and ritual center for the Tiwanaku people. Similar to other ancient cultures, massive precisely cut stone blocks, some weighing as much as 400 tons, were used to build the temple. Instead of mortar, bronze cramps were often used to join and hold these massive blocks together. There are many similarities between the temple of Pumapunku at Tiwanaku and the Christian Church today. While the Tiwanaku laid the foundation for the Incan Empire, Christ has laid the foundation for the Church. Centered on the cross, and joined (clicking) with Christ our cornerstone, we are the living stones held together by the mortar of faith. Nowhere is this truth better expressed than Peter's first epistle.

> As you come to him, the living Stone—rejected by men but chosen by God and precious to him—you also, like living stones, are being built into a spiritual house to be a holy priesthood, offering spiritual sacrifices acceptable to God through Jesus Christ...But you are a chosen generation, a royal priesthood, a holy nation, His own special people, that you may proclaim the praises of Him who called you out of darkness into His marvelous light. (1 Peter 2:4-6, 9)

In the introduction of Chuck Colson's watershed book, *The Body*, he states,

> "[Our primary witness] is made by the people of God *being* the people of God, living in biblical fidelity in obedience to Christ's commands."[21]

As Christians we too often tend to focus solely on individual spiritual growth, and ignore the maturation of community. While personal maturity is critical it does not happen separated from the corporate spiritual growth of the body of Christ, the Church! The Church is the community of believers, and the place where corporate spiritual growth primarily takes place. Peter sees the spiritual growth of both the individual and the community happening in concert. The growth of the believer is intricately coupled with the growth of the body.

We are being built (maturing) into a spiritual house (1 Peter 2:4). A subtle, but important, point to note when reading these verses is that in every case Peter is using the first person plural. This means that wherever you see the word "you" he is actually saying "you all" (or y'all for our friends in the south). This exhortation is not for the "super" Christian, our pastor or small group leader. It is for all of us. Quoting the prophet Isaiah (Isa. 28:16), Peter announces that Christ is *the* living Stone, *the* cornerstone. The cornerstone is the first stone laid when constructing a building. The three dimensions of

---

[21] Chuck Colson, *The Body*, Dallas: Word Publishing, 1996, XIX.

the cornerstone define both the directions of the walls and their vertical alignment. The Church is the building that God desires to build. We are the living stones who take our direction and alignment from Jesus, our cornerstone. Our task as living stones is to stay in line with him.

Allow me a mini diversion here to share another note of interest (at least to me). The word Peter uses for stone here is neither *petros* nor *petra*. It is *lithos*. While *petra* would be a very large, rough rock (such as the rock that covered the tomb of Jesus, and *petros* would simply be a smaller rock or pebble *lithos* meant a stone already cut and prepared for use in building. The mammoth stones used to build the pyramids of Egypt or the Parthenon in Greece or Pumapunku would be *lithos*. I trust you see the analogy that Peter is communicating. As Christians we have been prepared, from *petros* to *lithos*. We have been cut and shaped. We are being formed into the very image of Christ, the cornerstone. As living stones we are being built into His spiritual house. The builder is God; Jesus is the foundation; and we are the building blocks carefully being constructed into the Church, the body of Christ.

Peter is not talking about a church building. There were no church buildings in the New Testament. We are the Church. And His Church is not static, not tied to a unique geographical location. The Church is dynamic, outward facing, moving as a holy nation, a royal priesthood (v. 9). Christianity is not simply a thing to be believed or a religion to be followed; it is a relationship to be lived . . .and shared. Christianity is the Church. It is to be built of living stones—the very lives of those who have become spiritually alive through faith in Jesus Christ. We cannot live in spiritual isolation. Faith is the mortar that connects us. We must be available to Him and to each other so that our Lord can use our lives to build the kingdom of Christ.

Are you part of the Church, the body of Christ, or are you out there on your own? In verses 9 and 10 Peter gives four clear characteristics for those who are living stones. First, we are a chosen people. As we discussed earlier, there is a mystery regarding whether we have believed in the Lord or He has chosen us. The truth of Scripture is that both are true. Second, we are a royal priesthood. We are part of the priesthood of all believers. All of us have been called to ministry (Eph. 4:11–13). All of us have both the joy and the responsibility of serving Christ and each other. What a sad indictment of our churches today that, as the anonymous quote states, "The great task of the Church is not only to get sinners into heaven, but to get saints out of bed." Third, we are citizens of a "holy nation". To belong to Christ is to belong to His kingdom. If we belong to Christ, we are citizens of His holy nation which is eternal. Finally, we are "His own special people". This marvelous fact has not come to reality by mere chance; it has been the plan of God for ages.

Nowhere have I seen the truth of the Church better exemplified than while I attended college. While I am sure this small church in central Illinois was not perfect, it was the body of Christ to me. And no two people at that church exemplified that better than Dan and Gayle Wilkinson. I was raised in a Christian home but in college drifted from a childhood faith that had not taken strong enough roots. It was not until my junior year that I again found myself regularly attending church. It was at this small church that I watched Dan and Gayle exemplify what it meant to be "living stones".

Dan was a gentle giant. A big man with a full beard and a forgiven past Dan had three loves: His Lord, his wife & family and Harleys. Granted, when I knew Dan he had yet to buy his Harley, but he loved motorcycles. To see Dan in full riding leathers coming down the road on his bike could be intimidating. However, his soft spoken voice, empathetic eyes and absolute love for the lost quickly overwhelmed any initial misgivings one would have. Dan was working out of the church as a Christian counselor, and it was in his home and his office that I would spend many an hour over the next three years growing in grace as I completed my graduate degree. Gayle Wilkinson was a full time student working on her doctorate degree in Education. She was the primary teacher of

It's Our Turn Now

our Sunday school class and exhibited a lot of patience as I "helped" Dan grout tile, paint bedrooms or hang mini-blinds in their home. Whether at church or while working together at their home God continued to speak to me through them both. Let me share one particular exchange with Gayle proved pivotal in my walk with Christ after college.

Like most churches they had the traditional reception for graduating students. However, this was a small church and when I graduated from college I was the only graduate to be honored. After the Sunday evening service we all migrated to the fellowship area for the traditional cake, punch and gift (usually a Bible or devotional) for the graduates. Over the past 18 months in that church, families had adopted me. I had quickly learned that if I waited long enough in the foyer some family would invite me over for a real Sunday dinner. During these same 18 months I had grown in my faith, but I was still struggling with the day-to-day temptations of college life. Long story short, that night I got my Bible . . .and a card. It was clear from the thickness of the envelope that it was filled with money. This was an unexpected twist. I opened the card and found nearly $500 dollars from a church of less than 100 middle class folks.

I felt overwhelmed, emotional and totally undeserving of the love this small church continued to show me. Gayle came up and put her arm around me stating something I already fully knew, that the church loved me. I knew I had not been consistent in my walk and that I did not "deserve" the gift. I told her that I did not believe I could "repay" the church for what they had done for me. Gayle responded telling me something that I have never forgotten. She said, "Someday you will be able to do this for someone else. And when you do you will be paying us back."

It wouldn't be until I finished graduate school and began exploring career options that I fully grasped the depth of her words. I was home debating between two job offers in Los Angeles. One was my dream job, the Hughes Space and Communications Company, and the other TRW, Inc. I had only recently started listening to Christian music and a new artist, Steven Curtis Chapman, had quickly become my favorite. As I was driving through my hometown his "new" song, *My Turn Now,* came on. As I listened to the chorus, Gayle's words resonated in my mind. God had used Champaign First Church of the Nazarene to be Christ to me. Now it was my turn to be Christ to someone else. In that moment while driving my car God granted a peace to choose TRW over the dream offer from Hughes. It would be because of this career choice that I would meet my wife, but also choose to attend the church where I met Johnny and the many Laotian boys at New Life that I grew to love. It was my turn and God had already chosen His field where He was calling me to obediently serve.

    It would be several years later before I would find myself back in Dan and Gayle's home. They were living near St. Louis, Dan was continuing his counseling practice and Gayle was a professor at the University of Missouri - St. Louis. I spent the evening in their basement shooting pool with Dan and talking about a potential call to the ministry. I had no idea that two years later at the age of 47 Dan would be gone. As I write the final touches on this last chapter I am also 47 years old. During his 47 years Dan led 46 people to the Lord. I was one of them. Now it is your turn. Is anything stopping you? Maybe you feel unqualified. Maybe you feel that you have too much baggage. Maybe you feel you have no story. In all three cases you are wrong. Be a Dan Wilkinson. He, like so many others, is a wonderful example of what it means to "Click with God."

Index

1 Cor. 13	32	1 Peter 4	
1 Corinthians 2		16	39
6	52	1 Peter 5	
1 Corinthians 3		8	xiv
1	52	1 Samuel 13	
9	167	14	80
1 Corinthians 13		2 Chronicles 16	
9-12	64	9	82, 149
1 Corinthians 14		2 Corinthians 3	
20	52	18	63
1 Corinthians 15		2 Corinthians 5:7	142
21-22	114	2 Corinthians 5	
1 John 1		17	142
8-10	77	2 Samuel 6	
1 John 3		14-15	127
4	72	2 Samuel 12	
1 Kings 19:12	145	7	80
1 Kings 22		2 Timothy 3	
17	166	1-5	62
1Peter 1		Acts 1	
6	32	8	135, 140
1 Peter 2		Acts 11	
4	186	25-26	35
4-6	183, 186	26	39
9	186, 187	Acts 13	
9-10	187	22	80

Acts 26
  28 39
Arthur Erickson 25
Colossians 3
  9-11 77
Ecclesiastes 11
  6 173
Ephesians 1
  7-8 83
  17-20 158
Ephesians 2
  8 52
  8-9 .... 50, 111, 179
  8-10 78
  10 180
  15 77
Ephesians 4
  11-13 188
  13-14 52
  22-24 .... 57, 77
Ephesians 5
  1-2 28
  17 127
Exodus 20 .... 98, 101
  17 55
Ezra 3:8-13 139
Galatians 2
  2 149
Galatians 5
  22-23 122
  25 .... 123, 141
Galations 5:25 140
Gen 2
  9 157
Genesis 1
  27 75
  31 75
Genesis 3
  23-24 75

Genesis 5
  22-24 131
  24 132
Hebrew 12:1 140
Hebrews 1
  3-4 60
Hebrews 5
  13-14 52
Hebrews 10
  10 112
  14 .... 51, 52
Hebrews 12
  1 v
  2 124
  11 124
Isa. 28
  16 186
Isaiah 6
  3 132
  8 167
Isaiah 28
  16 183
James 1
  22 144
James 2
  19 49
James 4
  17 81
Jeremiah 23
  24 25
John 1
  12 50
John 3
  16 49
  16-18 79
John 8
  34 74
John 12
  25 157

Index

John 14
- 16-17 131
- 21 54
- 26 131

John 15
- 4 ....123, 140
- 4-8 124
- 5 ....117, 122
- 6-7 75
- 9 124
- 9-16 124
- 10 124
- 12-13 125
- 12-15 65
- 26 131

John 16
- 7-11 131
- 13-15 131

John 18
- 37-38 25

John 19
- 30 52

Joshua 24
- 15 95

Luke 10
- 29 161

Luke 23
- 19 103
- 22 103

Luke 24 120
- 21 120

Mark 3
- 6 39

Mark 4
- 1-9 177

Mark 8
- 34-35 65

Mark 11-12 100

Mark 12
- 13 39

Matt. 28
- 18-20 165

Matthew 4
- 8-9 133

Matthew 5
- 43-47 55
- 48 ....47, 49, 51, 55

Matthew 5-7 166
Matthew 5-9 166
Matthew 8-9 166

Matthew 9
- 36-37 166
- 37-38 166
- 38 167

Matthew 10 166

Matthew 11
- 28-30 66

Matthew 16 153
- 13-18 154
- 16 154
- 18 155

Matthew 17
- 12 155
- 24-26 156
- 25 157

Matthew 19
- 17 54
- 18 54
- 21 54

Matthew 21
- 18-22 103

Matthew 22
- 16 39
- 34-36 101
- 37-39 62
- 37-40 101
- 39 55

Matthew 24
- 51 ... 30

Matthew 28 ... 178
- 18-20 ... 167

Philippians 3
- 10 ... 99
- 10-11 ... 99
- 12 ... 53
- 12-16 ... 53
- 14 ... 100

Proverbs 8
- 17 ... 87

Proverbs 16
- 18 ... 57

Proverbs 20
- 9 ... 69

Proverbs 27
- 19 ... 60

Psalm 27
- 4 ... 99

Psalm 46
- 9-10 ... 134
- 10 ... 134

Psalm 77
- 1-3 ... xiii

Revelations 3
- 20 ... 121

Revelations 4
- 8 ... 132

Romans 2
- 1 ... 80

Romans 3
- 10 ... 76
- 11 ... 76
- 12 ... 76
- 21-31 ... 111
- 22-25 ... 111
- 23 ... 49, 76, 110

Romans 5
- 1-2 ... 105, 112
- 8 ... 49
- 12-21 ... 112, 113
- 19 ... 52

Romans 6
- 6 ... 77
- 23 ... 49, 110

Romans 7 ... 98, 143
- 25 ... 83

Romans 7
- 15-16 ... 67

Romans 8 ... 143
- 1-4 ... 84
- 28 ... 113, 114
- 30 ... 78

Romans 10
- 9 ... 111

Zechariah 4:6b ... 139